BOLD SEA STORIES

★★★ Marlin Bree books ★★★

"It is no accident that our history books are filled with adventures of the sea. Sailors and non-sailors are captivated by nautical stories. ...when reading this book, you will feel like you are onboard during some of the harshest calamities in recent history."— Gary Jobson, America's Cup racer and author

"A perilous tale."— *Minneapolis StarTribune*

"He was reasonably sure he'd not live to see the next day."— *St. Paul Pioneer Press*

"Bree and *Persistence* dared greatly, struggled greatly and had a worthy run, told with touching candor. Bree is at his best in telling of those times when the lake was at its worst." — *Evening Journal*, Wilmington, DE.

"...will appeal to readers interested in maritime history as well as to yachting enthusiasts." — *Publisher's Weekly*

"... a living recollection of one man's communication with that greater power everyone must someday face." — *Evening Telegram*, Superior, WI

"...Up from the pages emerges and aura of distance, dispersion, absences; a cleanliness and poetry; and above all, a cold windy presence determining all. Fascinating." — *Sail*

"Marlin Bree's first-hand knowledge of monster waves and survival has enabled him to vividly and accurately describe six true adventures in *Broken Seas*. The book details triumph and tragedy and is a must-read for sailors, and even landlubbers will enjoy these amazing tales."
— Chuck Luttrell, author of *Heavy Weather Boating Emergencies*

BOLD SEA STORIES

21 INSPIRING ADVENTURES

MARLIN BREE

MARLOR PRESS

St. Paul, Minnesota

BOLD SEA STORIES

Published by Marlor Press, Inc.

ISBN-13: 9781892147-35-6
ISBN-10: 1-892147-35-1
EAN: 978-1-4956-0095-1

Manufactured in the United States of America

Distributed to the book trade in the USA
By Independent Publishers Group, Chicago

MARLOR PRESS
4304 Brigadoon Drive • Saint Paul, MN 55126

Bold Sea Stories Series
First Edition

Library of Congress Cataloging-in-Publication Data

Names: Bree, Marlin, 1933- author.
Title: Bold sea stories : 21 inspiring adventures / Marlin Bree.
Description: First edition. | Saint Paul, Minnesota : Marlor Press, 2020. |
   Series: Bold sea stories series | Includes index.
Identifiers: LCCN 2019055153 (print) | LCCN 2019055154 (ebook) | ISBN
   9781892147356 (trade paperback) | ISBN 9781495600951 (ebook)
Subjects: LCSH: Sea stories. | Voyages and travels. | Shipwrecks.
Classification: LCC G525 .B811 2020 (print) | LCC G525 (ebook) | DDC
   910.4/5--dc23
LC record available at https://lccn.loc.gov/2019055153
LC ebook record available at https://lccn.loc.gov/2019055154

CONTENTS

For Loris,
who journeys
ahead of me

FOREWORD

Waves came like dark walls out of the night. His unprotected face was painfully cold. One boot had cracked and water had entered. It would be so easy to bend his head to his chest as if in prayer and let his little skiff rock him into slumber. Looking down, he saw ice coating his oilskins. Ice encased his feet; icicles hung from his fingertips. The Old Man knew that if the ice coating got too thick, his boat would become top-heavy and roll over in the waves. To sleep was to die.

Helmer Aakvik, of Hovland, Minnesota, fought a deadly storm on Lake Superior and became a legend. His tale is a sea adventure that I am privileged to report in "The Old Man and the Inland Sea: A classic tale of survival." (Pages 1–14. Also, pages 193–194)

It is a stirring, poignant tale of how a brave old man survived the worst that the inland sea could throw at him and his old skiff. Within this sea tale are insights into his thoughts and feelings and how he handled himself and his boat to survive. There were some surprises for me: At midnight, during the height of the ice storm, when the winds howled across the open seas, he reported he felt comfortable as he waited out the dawn. He was frozen to his seat.

The "Old Man" is one of my favorite sea narratives. For years, I have searched for the legends and the lore of the world's wickedest waters, from the North Atlantic to the South Pacific, as well as upon (and under the dark depths) of the world's largest freshwater sea.

In my home-built sailboat, *Persistence*, I have sailed in the wake of ship-wrecks. On a dive boat, I was with shipwreck hunters "mowing the lawn" to check out an underwater sighting of a lost vessel, a "ghost ship." I have interviewed brave captains, waterfront people, divers, and maritime experts.

Most sea stories will inspire you; some might make you feel like shedding a tear. The 21 chapters vary in subject and in length. You can read most in about 15 to 25 minutes. This is a goodly length of time if you are on your boat and at anchor or tied up at a dock, and you want to relax with a little reading matter.

Boating Writers International honored two tales, The Old Man and the Inland Sea, and The Day Superior Went Wild, with the top awards the writer's organization can present to a boating writer: the BWI Grand Prize

Writing Awards.

Some articles originated from my newspaper stories, a lot from boating magazines, and some from my books such as *Wake of the Green Storm* or *In the Teeth of the Northeaster*. You can learn more in the Appendix's Publication History and Awards (p. 187). Another section, Author's Notes, tells more about the adventures or updates information. It also reports about the boats they sailed. I don't comment on all stories, just the ones in which I feel I can add a dimension.

Boats play a significant part in my narratives. They are often the unsung heroes of a sea story's adventures, struggling as if alive to save their skippers. A fellow sailor will understand.

• A 10-foot plywood boat sets sail from California to cross 7,800 miles of the Pacific Ocean (Ten Feet Across the Pacific). A storm hits. Can the tiny craft survive?

• An old 17-foot skiff gets caught in an ice storm as its elderly skipper searches for a lost friend—and both nearly end up as blocks of ice (The Old Man and the Inland Sea).

• An ore boat races full ahead toward a distant shore after a reef tears out her bottom. Will the *Edmund Fitzgerald* find a safe harbor before she sinks? (The Last Race of the *Edmund Fitzgerald*)

• On the stormy North Atlantic, a Viking ship struggles against heavy seas to return to Norway (Ship of Dreams). Will it make it "home?"

• A Civil War-era schooner sitting on the bottom for 150 years, intact, and appearing ready to sail away, is discovered by amateur scuba divers. Can they bring this incredible find back to the surface? (The Ghost Ship from 19 Fathoms)

All stories are true—real people, real boats, real events. These are adventures full of heroic courage, inspired ingenuity, and remarkable determination. They resonate in your mind and your heart. They live on viscerally.

Welcome to Bold Sea Stories.

—Marlin Bree
Shoreview, Minnesota

Also by Marlin Bree

DEAD
ON THE
WIND

BROKEN SEAS

WAKE
OF THE
GREEN STORM

IN THE TEETH
OF THE
NORTHEASTEER

CALL
OF THE
NORTH WIND

BOAT LOG
& RECORD

THE DANGEROUS
BOOK FOR BOATERS

ALONE
AGAINST
THE ATLANTIC
By Gerry Spiess with Marlin Bree

1

The old man and the inland sea

———————————————— ☆☆☆ ————————————————

A classic tale of survival

AT 8:30 A.M., HELMER AAKVIK PEERED OUT the window of his ramshackle cabin overlooking Lake Superior. The lake was steaming with dense fog banks forty feet high, a bad sign. Though he could not see them, he knew waves were kicking up further out on Superior's notorious open waters.

He would not go out to his nets today.

The 62-year-old Aakvik settled down at his kitchen table to enjoy a second cup of strong coffee when his neighbor, Elmer Jackson, came trudging over. The cabin door opened with a blast of wind.

Jackson was blunt: "The young fellow is still out on his boat."

The Old Man looked up, troubled. The storm coming on had an off-shore wind from the north-northwest. It was one of the worst kinds.

He abruptly put down his coffee cup. "Call the Coast Guard."

Jackson took a deep breath. "Just don't you go out."

.... ❊ ....

Grabbing a jacket and cap, the Old Man walked down the winding path to the bluff's edge. A steady wind knifed out of the northwest; the temperature was dropping. This was late November in the North Country; soon there'd be ice and snow.

On a rock ledge jutting above the lake, the Old Man came to the wooden fish house that he and Carl Hammer shared. In the open end of the shed, Hammer's boat was still missing.

He checked around. Sure enough, the young fisherman had helped himself to Aakvik's gas supply. The borrowing was OK. In fact, they shared supplies all the time in this close-knit Norwegian community.

But the Old Man had an old Lockport and an elderly Johnson outboard. Hammer used a newer Johnson, which needed about a half a quart of oil mixed in five gallons of gas. Aakvik's old two-cycles required twice that amount of oil. A too-heavy oil-gas ratio would gum up his young friend's carburetor and foul his spark plugs. This would stall his engine.

Hefting the can, he swirled the gas around. He could see drops of water come to the surface. The gas was old and had accumulated condensation. The old man's normal routine was to filter the water out of the gas so it didn't freeze in the lines and kill the engine.

Hammer hadn't filtered his gas.

.... ❀ ....

The Old Man hurried back to his cabin and dressed himself in layers of wool: socks, underwear, pants and shirt. Wool was the key to survival on Superior because it could keep him warm even when it was wet. Over his wool, he pulled on his "oilies," a heavy rubber fisherman's suit, adding rubber boots, wool mitts and a sheepskin helmet. Aakvik never went out on that lake, winter or summer, without a good set of oilies.

He told everyone in his broken English, "they saved your life."

.... ❀ ....

At about 9 a.m., the Old Man stood atop the rock outcropping over the slide. His 17-foot long skiff was tied to a wooden slide about 30 feet above the water, located high above the shoreline rocks. The slide was made up of three trimmed tree trunks, each about eight to ten inches in diameter, and over forty feet long. Today, there would be no problem launching the skiff. The wind was blowing off the land, and not from the water.

He thought for a moment, then threw an ax into his boat. He added two more pieces of equipment: an old 50-pound wooden fish crate and fifty fathoms of rope.

The Old Man used a hand-cranked winch to lower his skiff down the boat slide and into the water. As he hefted himself aboard, the small skiff bobbed up and down as if to welcome his familiar weight. He settled himself on his seat, a heavy wooden plank in front of the transom. He sat upright, open to the wind and the spray. His outboard engine was behind him.

The Old Man felt comfortable. He told friends that he felt more at home aboard his boat than he did in his own living room.

He had built his own boat. The Old Man picked out the timber himself in his nearby north woods. A skiff took him about 3 to 4 weeks to build and he never painted it. The boat wouldn't win any beauty prizes.

The slab-sided hull allowed a fisherman to lean over the side and pull in a net without the boat tipping over. The hull was heavy. In wooden boats, heavy meant strong.

At over 20 years old, the Old Man's boat was beyond a North Shore fishing boat's normal working years. It was tired: the skiff had punched through countless waves and survived many storms. Many times, the Old Man had dragged it groaning with a hold full of fish up the log slide. It had rot in some bottom planks. Some of the fastenings holding the planks to the frames felt a little loose.

But the Old Man had faith. His skiff had taken him out and brought him back every time. It could be relied upon one more time.

The first blasts of the offshore wind sliced into him once he left the shore. Out here, the wind was coming up and the seas were starting to build. He'd have to hurry. The temperature was about six degrees above zero and it was dropping.

Atop a wave, he saw the first marker buoy flag. Moments later, he could make out a line of bobbing buoys, strung out in a row, their line bending in the wind and the waves.

The Kid was not here.

Aakvik made a run alongside the line, being careful not to foul his propeller on the nets. At the end marker buoy, Aakvik scanned the horizon. The big lake was alive. Away from shore, the waves continued to build; his small boat bobbed up and down. He held his cupped hands to his eyes to give him better vision. Still no sign of Hammer or his skiff.

One thing was certain: the young fisherman had not tied his boat to the marker buoys. Heavy rock anchors held these buoys to the bottom. If a fishing boat had engine trouble, the fisherman could hang on to a buoy to await rescue.

The Old Man pulled his boat alongside the final buoy. He grabbed it for a moment and turned off his engine.

And waited.

.... ❀ ....

Along the bluffs on shore, watchers with binoculars scanned the broken seas. The heavy rollers of Superior were high and mean, with waves rearing to become the lake's notorious "square rollers." The wind was coming up and blowing the fog around in patches.

Word had spread. The village knew that the Old Man had gone out to bring in The Kid.

Someone recognized Aakvik's old boat bounding up and down in the waves. He hung onto a buoy with his hands.

Minutes passed. They saw his boat move away from the nets. From the way his boat was handling, they could tell he was drifting, without power.

The Old Man was in trouble.

.... ❀ ....

The Old Man was moving with the waves and the wind. He had turned off his engine. The Kid had a problem with his motor and was drifting. Without power, the Old man would be carried in the same direction.

He prayed he'd be in time.

The wind speed was about 38 mph. He went down into the trough of one wave, then bounded upward. Moving walls of water surrounded him.

Once he had his bearings on the speed and direction his partner was drifting, he fired up his engine and began motoring downwind. When he was seven or eight miles out, he let his boat idle atop a wave for one last look around for his missing partner. At this height, he could see for miles atop the tumbling seas. But there was no sign of Hammer.

The waves whistled as they roared past his skiff. He'd never heard them that noisy before.

There was nothing more he could accomplish out here. It was time to return to shore.

In the fog, he could not see the tall headlands of home. Since he had been running downwind, he could find his way to shore by reversing his course and powering upwind.

That meant turning his boat around and plunging back into the face of the mounting wind and waves.

Suddenly, his roaring outboard started to splutter. Then it died.

In the eerie silence, the Old Man turned. His outboard was white with ice.

.... ✸ ....

It was the Lockport. He had been using the elderly outboard without its cover, as he often did. The entire engine had been splashed with spray and the water had frozen. Ice encrusted the entire engine.

He wound the starting chord. Turning the throttle to start, he gave the outboard a hard pull; the old engine wheezed several times. Again, and again, he ran through the starting drill. But the ice-encrusted engine would not fire into life.

He sat back for a moment, weary. He was thankful he had the foresight to bring his spare engine onboard. The newer 14-horsepower Johnson lay sloshing in the water on the floorboard.

In the storm-filled seas, he'd have to wrestle the heavy Lockport off the transom. Timing his movements between waves, he unscrewed the clamps that held the Lockport to the transom and grunted: he couldn't move it. the outboard was frozen to the boat. He hefted his weight against the hundred-pound engine, felt the ice break, and, leaned over to grasp the power head. He pulled hard; the old outboard came out of the water. Carefully, the Old Man lowered it into the bottom of the boat.

Cradling it like a baby, he pulled the Johnson out of the bilge. His boat and his salvation depended on this engine

There could be no mistakes now. He braced himself to lower the power head onto its clamps. With a final slide, the outboard was on the transom. The small boat reacted to the extra weight and drag, cocking broadside to the wind.

He wiped his face and discovered that perspiration had turned to ice. His hat had a rime of white around it.

The Old Man snicked the outboard's gear into neutral, pulled the choke button and twisted the throttle to the starting position. He yanked on the starter chord. Hard.

There was not even an encouraging whuff or slight backfire.

His second engine wouldn't start.

In his T-35 jet trainer, Major Leo Tighe scanned the surface of wind-churned Superior. It would be difficult to pick out a small boat from the white caps. A hit-and-run snowstorm had come up from nowhere, racing with unusual speed out of the northwest, and dumped 13 inches of snow on the ground. Freezing rain and sleet turning to ice had blanketed the Duluth airport and the rest of the Midwest.

He had been lucky to get in the air.

Riding with him in the back seat was Lt. Gerald Buster. Flying in a north-south search pattern, fierce winds buffeted them. More than once, they came closer to Superior's outstretched fingers than they cared to.

"There!"

Major Tighe had spotted something in the waves below. He circled.

At 2 p.m., about 20 miles from shore, they saw a small, white boat.

On their first pass, it looked like it was under power. The man in the boat's rear seat payed no attention to their low-flying jet.

They circled again, this time lower yet, and, saw that the man's engine wasn't putting out any wake, nor was the boat making any progress in the waves. The boat was rolling broadside to the wave trains. This was a dangerous position.

The man was in trouble, but he wouldn't look up or signal to them. The boat and the man were white. It dawned on Major Tighe: both were coated in ice.

He circled so that a radar station onshore could get a fix and relay the information to the Coast Guard. Low on fuel, he returned to the Duluth air base. There wasn't anything else he could do from the air.

A rogue wave reared over the boat, swamping it and filling his craft a quarter full of water. The Old Man bailed—but his boat was riding too low in the water.

He laid his hands on his Lockport and felt a twinge of regret wash over him: the old engine had been his fishing partner for many years; he'd taken it to the Hovland blacksmith shop to have it welded when it had broken. There was a bond between the old outboard and the Old Man.

Reluctantly, he threw it overboard.

His skiff was lighter by over a hundred pounds. The freeboard lifted an inch or two. He began bailing again, trying to keep pace with the spray and spume that came aboard. When the water was down to the floorboards, he turned his attention to his one remaining outboard.

He took off his gloves, baring his skin to the frozen metal, and twisted the gas line off by hand. No gas came out. His fuel had frozen solid. There had been water in his gas.

The old fisherman stuck the gas line in his mouth. The raw rubber, soaked in gasoline, made him gag. Inch by inch, he moved the gas line through his mouth, warming it. After about a half an hour, he blew hard on one end. The ice block popped out. The gas flowed: the line was free.

He reattached the gas line to the engine and hauled on the starter chord. With a roar, the Johnson came to life. They began their run back to shore.

The short November day was ending. It was growing dark.

The oncoming waves were 20 feet high, dwarfing his boat. Punching into them, the old skiff took a terrible pounding. Its planks were flexing; some looked like they were separating. Fastenings were loosening.

The storm was too much for the old boat.

There was nothing to do but turn off the engine. The moment the motor stopped; he noticed the awful noise of the sea once more. Wind howled across his open boat and white-crested growlers reared in front of him.

Without power, his boat cocked sideways to the waves, a dangerous sea-keeping position. Breakers sloshed over its sides.

Reaching down, he picked the rope out of the half-frozen slurry and tied it to the wooden fishing crate. Grunting with the effort, he hefted the crate over the side. With a splash, it sank part way into the waves; he saw it float away from his drifting boat.

When he felt a tug on the rope, he tied the line off the bow. The boat's bow swung around to the waves.

His improvised sea anchor was holding; his boat was riding to the waves with her bow cocked at a slight angle to them—

her best sea-keeping position.

He had done all he could. Now he could only bow his head at the growing fury of the storm.

.... ❋ ....

Back in Hovland, the families grew desperate. Atop the cliff, they could look out at the seas and imagine the ordeal of their men in the open boats. They shared a sense of helplessness.

"What could you do on shore?" Helmer Aakvik's wife, Christine, wondered aloud.

They had called the sheriff, but snow and high winds kept his float-plane from searching the storm-filled lake. From Grand Marais, the Coast Guard's small boat came out to search, but turned back when its engine lost power. The gas line was freezing up.

About 20 miles away near Isle Royale, the steel Coast Guard cutter, *Woodrush*, got an emergency call. It responded by steaming hard toward Hovland, into the teeth of the storm.

In the meantime, the Coast Guard sent another lifeboat to Hovland. When the 36-foot lifeboat arrived, it was riding six to eight inches lower in the water because of the weight of the ice that covered the boat. They had been fighting a Number 6 Sea. Waves averaged 15 feet in height.

After chopping off ice, they searched up and down the shoreline, try-ing to estimate where the lost fishermen might have drifted. The lifeboat had no radar. The crewmen had to scan the waves by eye—an almost im-possible job in the spray and ice. By evening, when they called off their search, the wind howled at 50 miles per hour.

The *Woodrush* kept on station, but temperatures neared the zero mark. The winds were increasing, and, so were the seas. Ice built on its top-sides, making the *Woodrush* top-heavy and in danger of capsizing. Several times, they returned to harbor to chop off the ice.

Along the shore, in the little fishing community, people prayed that the Old Man and the Kid, each huddled alone in their open boats, would survive the night.

.... ❋ ....

Waves came like dark walls out of the night. They rose high and crashed into the old boat; he heard its groans; he could feel its agony.

The Old Man had been out sixteen hours, and he had nothing to eat or drink. His face and his hands were raw and painful from the cold. His foot grew numb where a boot had cracked and water came in. The Old Man's mind was growing slack with fatigue.

If the ice built too much, his boat would get top heavy and roll over in the waves. Thankful he had taken his ax along, the Old Man chopped ice and threw chunks off his boat.

During the long night, his mind drifted. He tried to figure out what happened. In his rush to get out to his nets early that morning, The Kid probably just tossed on his usual work clothes. Tomorrow was Thanksgiving Day, a festive time in the small Norwegian community. It would be a special holiday since Carl and his wife were expecting a baby. The Kid figured he'd be out there before any storm came up, pick his nets and get back, just as he had done thousands of times before. He wouldn't be long; there was no need for special precautions. Carl didn't wear his oilskins to protect him from the cold and the spray.

The Old Man bent his head. Cold and fatigued, shivering in some stage of hypothermia, Carl just slumped down finally and went to sleep. Without power, his boat cocked sideways to the waves. Top heavy with ice, it rolled over. His partner's end was quick, or he prayed it was.

The Old Man dared not sleep. It would be easy to slump in his wooden seat, let his head bow down to his chest, and allow the motion of the skiff rock him into slumber.

To sleep was to die.

He roused himself. Off in the distance, flashes of light bounced off the headlands of Hovland and Chicago Bay. That would be his rescuers, he thought. There was no way to tell them he was further out from shore. A lot further.

Ice was everywhere. It covered his skiff. When he looked down, he saw that it coated his oilskins. Ice encased his feet; icicles hung from his fingertips.

During the night, the moon came out. The Old Man admired the beauty of the spray by moonlight. It glistened white, surreal and ethereal around him.

He saw something gleaming white in the water.
Ice surrounded his boat.

At dawn, heavy steam covered the lake. The Old Man scanned the horizon, but he couldn't locate the high, dark hills above Hovland. His boots had frozen to the bottom of the boat; he couldn't get up or move around to chop the ice. The bow glistened with ice a foot thick.

He turned: ice sheeted his outboard, including the flywheel. The starter rope was frozen hard.

He took off his mitts. With his uncovered hands, he worked the starter rope into flexibility. The Old Man wound two strands around the metal starting pulley. He kept his fingers moving so they would not freeze to the metal. The strands just fit.

He put mitts back on his numb hands. He waited a moment, said a silent prayer, and yanked. With a puff of blue smoke, the engine chuffed into life.

Heavy with ice, the skiff rode eight inches lower in the water, its bow barely lifting to the waves. With little reserve buoyancy left, his boat could sink if a single wave came aboard. He bailed constantly; he nursed his engine for six hours.

When he was within sight of land, his hopes lifted. He would make it yet. But six miles from shore, this engine stalled and quit.

He checked his fuel supply. Out of gas.

He hated what he had to do. Loosening the setscrews, he hefted the outboard off its mount and watched as the Johnson slipped beneath the waves. But the boat was lighter.

The shoreline was tantalizingly close. He could not give up.

It was Thanksgiving Day. The Coast Guard boat widened its search, crisscrossing the area. As it plowed through one bank of fog and into another, the temperature hovered around zero degrees.

"There!" someone yelled.

Off in the distance, something white and ice-covered bobbed up above the layer of lake steam.

As they steered nearer, they could make out what looked like a man's head. His face and beard glistened with frost and his hat was coated with white. His oilskins were encased in ice.

He rode low in a swamped boat that was itself a block of ice.

It was the Old Man.

He had not heard them approach. Suddenly, he saw the looming bow of the Coast Guard's boat headed toward him. He blinked, thinking it was a delusion, until the bow nudged his boat with a bump.

He tried to get up but he was frozen to his wooden seat. His ice-encrusted boots were frozen to the floorboards.

With care, the Coast Guard crew members chopped him out of the ice and lifted him from his skiff. When he was aboard, they fed him hot coffee—his first drink in 29 hours.

They tried to tow the Old Man's skiff home. But the old boat was so heavy with ice and so weak after its battles that it only lifted its bow a little and went under. They had to cut the rope. It sank down into the dark waters, lost forever.

As they came into Hovland's harbor, cheering rolled across the waves.

The Old Man looked around, amazed. "There must have been a hundred people."

Though he was having trouble moving, he still shrugged off offers of help. "I can still walk," he said. "I'm no cripple."

He protested when they placed him on a stretcher and a doctor gave him a preliminary examination. The doctor wanted to rush him to the hospital in Two Harbors.

"As if I needed a hospital," the Old Man snorted. "I only froze two toes."

He gulped an egg sandwich and drank a pint of hot coffee.

He declined a helicopter ride and insisted on riding sitting up in the ambulance.

The hospital treated him for frozen toes and frostbite. A doctor pronounced him as being in excellent shape, with normal blood pressure.

News people interviewed him. One asked if he prayed to his God for help during the long night. "No," he said, "there's some things a man has to do for himself."

Few words were as sweet to the Old Man as those of his neighbor, Elmer Jackson. Before Aakvik went out on his long search, Jackson had worried about him and the oncoming storm. The Old Man had promised Jackson: "Don't you worry, the Old Man will be back."

In the hospital, Elmer Jackson came to the Old Man's bedside and said: "You are a man of your word."

.... ❀ ....

It was years later that The Old Man returned to his cabin atop the rocky cliffs and what he considered "his home," Lake Superior. It surprised the small community when he ordered a wooden coffin built by a local boatbuilder.

He kept his coffin in his cabin, sometimes on his bed. The Old Man told people he was ready when his time came and that he had nothing to worry about. "I got my boat ready for the trip."

He tried it on for size; sometimes he slept in it. He reported that everything was just right. "I've seen quite a bit in my lifetime," he said, adding, "It's about time to go aloft, like the old sailors say."

.... ❀ ....

I headed off Hwy. 61 going north and climbed in third gear into the wooded hills overlooking Superior. The small cemetery was at the top surrounded by tall pine trees. The sun was down at a slant in the late afternoon, casting long shadows into the grass and onto the small tombstones.

Three weeks after he returned to Superior, the Old Man had died at age 90. He was buried at Trinity Lutheran Church Cemetery.

It was not hard to find the final resting place of the Old Man, near the pine trees at the northern edge. Today, a light wind swept through the foliage, rustling the pine branches.

His granite headstone recorded that he had been born 18 August 1896 and had died 11 January 1987. On it were the words:

> ***Home from the cruel sea***
> ***and in a peaceful harbor.***

I looked at the earth below my feet and I knew what was down there: Helmer was resting at last in his plain wooden coffin, nothing fancy. It was fitted with rope handles. His name was carved on the coffin lid.

He had two unusual additions. The boatbuilder had fitted the Old Man's coffin with a keel. And a compass rose.

That was so the Old Man could "steer a straight course to the stars." ☸

2

Ship of dreams

A Viking boat comes home

ROBERT ASP, A JUNIOR HIGH SCHOOL COUNSELOR from Moorhead, Minnesota, began his boat in 1971 by going into the north woods to pick out trees to furnish the timber. After cutting down 100 white oak trees, he trimmed them and dragged the logs to a local sawmill, where he had the oak ripped into planks.

Asp rented an unused potato warehouse. A perfectionist, the elderly boat builder wanted his boat to be as close as he could to the specifications of the 1,000-year-old Viking ships. He followed the ancient shipbuilder's techniques, except for the use of some power tools.

He often worked alone in the dark, unheated building. The ship's general details matched those of the original Viking ships. The oak keel was 15 inches thick. He built his hull with planks of one-inch thick oak, lapped one atop the other. By hand, he drove in 7,000 rivets, one at a time. The boat grew to 76 1/2-feet and had a 17-foot beam—a massive, magnificent vessel. It weighed 20 tons.

The name he gave his boat was the *Hjemkomst*. It meant, "the homecoming."

What the teacher wanted to do was sail his Viking vessel out of Lake Superior and across the North Atlantic, all the way back to Norway and the home of his ancestors. It would carry the dream that he and other immigrants had brought with them to the north woods and the shores of Lake

Superior.

In 1980, the old boat builder launched his vessel on Superior to test her for the long voyage ahead. But as his boat grew stronger, he grew weaker. The long years of working alone in an unheated potato warehouse were taking their toll.

A few months after his vessel's keel touched the icy waters of Superior, the old man died of leukemia. The vessel went into storage.

.... ❀ ....

When the *Hjemkomst* was trucked to Minneapolis to be a part of a festival, I was invited to go on board along with sailor Gerry Spiess. The *Hjemkomst* sat upon green grass, her varnished oak hull still gleaming.

"You wanted to cross the North Atlantic by small boat," Gerry challenged me. "They're looking for a crew."

Down below, cracks had formed in her massive keel. Her bilge was open to the rains and had water pooling in it; laminated pieces had split where epoxy glue had not held. There were cracks in some planks that worried me.

I saw holes in the hull's sides so that the crew could row when the wind failed.

"How high are these above the water line?"

A crewmember held up his hand to measure. "About 12 inches."

I swallowed hard. On one passage to England, a North Atlantic storm had sprung up and in the grip of the waves, the large steel ship I was on had been thrown about. Water had gushed down the deck—and that deck was at least 50 feet from the water. These oar holes, just inches above the waterline, could sink the *Hjemkomst*.

The whole project looked shaky. An amateur boat builder built this vessel under the most primitive of conditions—an unheated potato warehouse. He had no actual boat plans. The boat was of an ancient design that no one knew much about, or how to sail.

"Want to volunteer?"

"I'll pass on this one," I said. Not only did I not want to go, but I grew concerned for the crew.

Yet the dream lingered. It was not just any ship—it was a Viking vessel. The Vikings were among the most able seafarers in the world, voyaging to the ends of the earth as they knew it. Braving the North Atlantic, they had established a colony in the New World 500 years before Columbus discovered it for the rest of Europe.

I tried to imagine what it would have been like onboard. The vessel was open to the skies: every bit of rain, every storm, every rogue wave must have tormented the men on her decks. There would have been no escape, either: the vessel had no cabins, no below-deck quarters. In fact, there wasn't any real below-decks.

Some said Asp had chosen the wrong design. The graceful lines of the *Hjemkomst* came not from the hard-voyaging vessels of Viking lore and history, but from the Gokstad funeral boat. He had picked the sweeping, almost sensuous lines of a 1,000-year-old vessel that had been unearthed from a funeral mound and was now preserved in a museum in Norway. That boat's function was to be a bearer of the body of a Viking chieftain—a grave ship for his Viking burial. It was not meant to put to sea.

What the old boat builder should have built was the bluff-bowed, deeper and wider Viking raider ship, the drakkar. This had been the long ship that had carried the Vikings across the North Sea.

Asp's family—his wife, Rose, and their sons and daughter—knew nothing about handling the ancient Viking ship their father created.

But they had caught the dream of the old boatbuilder. They vowed that somehow the *Hjemkomst* would sail to Norway.

.... ❈ ....

Across the seas, Erik Rudstrom, age 61, heard the story of the north wood's homecoming boat. He was the master of a femboring, the modern-day derivative of the ancient Viking design, and had sailed one from Norway to Iceland.

Under Capt. Rudstrom's skilled hands, with the Asp family and friends as a crew, the *Hjemkomst* began her sea trials in Superior's chill waters. She could sail, but needed modifications.

They hauled her ashore in a little marina carved into a rocky promontory on Superior's north shore. The crew spent one summer rebuilding her massive keel with heavy steel bolts and deepening it by 12 inches. They plugged oar holes with coverings they could unfasten when they needed to row. They massively rebuilt the tiller and the rudder.

The crew lengthened the single mast. Now the Hjemkomst could spread more canvas to catch the trade winds of the North Atlantic. They added a topsail. Down below, in the shallow bilge, the crew stowed eight tons of Superior's granite rocks for ballast. The weight would help her stand up in a blow.

The crew worked up to 16 hours a day, readying their father's dream. A reporter who visited them noticed they had lobster-red hands from the cold, and that their layers of wool military uniforms, purchased because they were inexpensive but warm, smelled like dead fish.

By now, there were 13 in the crew, including three of Bob Asp's sons, Roger, Tom and Doug, and a daughter, Deborah Asp. There was the Norwegian skipper, Erik Rudstrom, and two other sailors from Norway who had come to Superior's shore to share the dream, Bjorn Holtet and Vegard Heide. There was Mark Hilde, Jeff Solum, Dennis Morken, Lynn Halmrast, Paul Hesse, and Myron Anderson.

Some say there was a 14th member: the old boatbuilder himself, Bob Asp.

·················· � ··················

If they had any doubts about the ship, they kept it to themselves. They believed that the hand of the dead builder had not erred and that his vision would live. The *Hjemkomst* would take on three great lakes across half a continent before she could sail the North Atlantic 3,500 miles to Oslo, Norway.

But first, the Viking ship had to cross Lake Superior. The old boat builder Bob Asp once said, "we were all kind of scared of it. "

The vessel was open to the skies and the seas. Waves could board the long, undecked vessel, sending her and her crew to a watery grave. She was not self-bailing, as modern sailing designs are. If any water came on board, it went straight into the shallow bilge instead of running overboard.

Captain Rudstrom had no illusions about Lake Superior, calling it a "sea." The skipper was concerned about Superior's unforgiving ways on an untested ship and an untried crew. He received advice: hug the coastline and be ready to duck into port whenever Superior's storms threatened on the horizon. Especially, a northeaster.

The Norwegian skipper was not inclined to pay attention to storm stories.

"We will go straight across the middle of the sea," he announced.

The voyage began from Superior's North Shore on May 11, 1982. Their departure from the Knife River harbor had been delayed because of easterly winds—the square-rigged _Hjemkomst_ could not sail into them. After the winds shifted to a northwesterly direction, the vessel began its monumental voyage.

Superior soon lived up to its reputation. The second night out, the wind switched to the northeast to become a northeaster. The crew found out what that meant

Bjorne Holtet was asleep inside a tent-like structure behind the mast when he found himself "swimming around" in his sleeping bag. A wave had come on board, swept across the deck and surged inside the tent where Bjorne lay sleeping.

Floundering about, he jumped out on deck. The night watch had over-canvassed the boat and was pushing it too hard in 20-to-30-knot winds. The boat's rail was dipping below the waves, scooping up solid green water.

The ship was in danger.

Reefing the sail, the crew straightened her up a precious few degrees. The weather rail came out of the water. They pumped the bilge and sailed on.

Exhausted and wet, the off-duty shift crawled back into their damp sleeping bags to get what comfort they could.

They had passed their second night on Superior.

.... ※ ....

The _Hjemkomst_ speeded eastward under gray skies. As they passed the Apostle Islands, their course led northeast, up and around the Keweenaw Peninsula, and into the teeth of the May wind. Far from going straight across the middle of the sea, as the captain had planned, they began a series of tacks, back and forth in a zig-zag pattern.

They pumped the bilge, then moved some ballast rocks from the bow to the stern. This raised the forward part of the hull a little so it would ride higher and deflect waves and spray coming aboard. They stuffed sealant into the oar holes to keep water out.

The open boat was pure misery. There was no heat on board.

To warm the small canvas tent, they had a compact stove. But the stove burned coal, not charcoal briquettes. They were supposed to start a fire using kindling. A small oversight: no one had brought kindling. They could not light their stove.

They came close to losing Igor, their dragonhead, when a wave knocked it down.

The boat's long keel made it difficult to maneuver. They had problems tacking high enough to clear Michigan's Keweenaw Peninsula. The square sail was difficult to set right; it didn't want to power into the wind.

For days, they tacked back and forth, zigzagging against persistent headwinds and rain squalls. Drenching rain and Superior's 38-degree-water kept them wet; they began to fantasize over hot meals of steaks and eggs.

On the morning of the May 18, eight days after leaving the western shores of Superior, they reached the southeastern tip of the lake and entered the locks at the Sault Ste Marie. They were off Superior, ending their ordeal.

Because of the stubborn headwinds and a northeaster, one crew member estimated that instead of covering about 400 miles, they had sailed close to 700.

Later, a crewmember said that the voyage across Lake Superior was the toughest part of the entire trip.

························ ❀ ····················

Crossing Lake Huron was a breeze. They whipped their Viking ship down the lake in around 30 hours of sailing.

By now, the cities of the Great Lakes had caught the spirit of the Viking vessel. Bells and whistles greeted the replica Viking ship as it entered ports with pennants flying at the masthead. Crowds cheered.

The *Hjemkomst* dashed across Lake Erie to the Erie Canal. A rowing club showed up, volunteering to row the vessel through the canal. In Albion, New York, school classes were let out to watch the vessel as it glided along the canal.

Hjemkomst crew members blew the Viking horn as the ship neared a bridge; from atop, well-wishers lowered baskets of fruit, food, or wine. From one bridge came a shower of T-shirts imprinted with the cryptic, Viking Valhalla Room.

One day, the ham radio operator on board, Jeff Solum, came out of his "radio room" inside the tent to get a message from another ham operator atop a bridge. The message was tied to a rock, then dropped. It hit Solem atop his head. It glanced off; he was unhurt.

.... �֎ ....

Pennants flying, the *Hjemkomst* sailed down the Hudson River to New York City. Her berth would be one of honor: New York City's historic South Street Seaport, on the East River.

Helicopters flew overhead. Blasts of air filled the sail from different directions, making it difficult for the helmsman to steer.

"Look out!" Someone shouted,

With a cracking noise, the ship collided with a steel bridge piling.

A heavy oak plank had cracked partway along its length on the port side. This was a major structural damage to the hull. But it was above the water line.

The ship put in at the South Street Seaport in lower Manhattan, in the shadows of the skyscrapers. The seaport's historic ships' massive hulls and giant masts dwarfed the smaller wooden ship.

.... ✖ ....

They braved Superior, crossed the Great Lakes and made it to the Big Apple. And here the voyage began to go wrong.

A fire broke out as the crew members prepared lunch: the diesel stove had flared up. Ship's master Roger Asp's right forearm caught fire. As he fell to the deck, a crew member poured water on him to douse the fire: scalding hot water to heat hot dogs. The crew member also had burns on his leg.

The crew worked on the ship. Instead of replacing the cracked planking, they decided to "sister" the damaged area by fastening another plank over it. This "doubling" braced the strake from the inside. They hoped the fastening would hold across the Atlantic.

There was a last problem. Crewmember Lynn Halmrast was on

shore to buy a going-away gift to send to his son. But as he held the miniature ship in his hand, turning it over, fear struck him. He began to worry that this could be the last toy he'd ever buy for his son.

With tears in his eyes, he made his difficult decision: He would leave the voyage. He would not be a hero, but he would return home and be a father to his son.

The crew now numbered 12.

.... ❈ ....

With their Viking figurehead guiding the way, they sailed out of New York harbor and entered the Atlantic Ocean. Their horizons now were open. They were sailors on a historic crossing of the North Atlantic in their father's Viking vessel. The sea they had feared now seemed the vessel's natural element, rather than its enemy. The boat began living up to its heritage.

Dark clouds overtook them; the barometer dropped. The wind increased to 40 knots. They encountered their first Atlantic storm.

By 1 a.m., the crew was roused to lower the square sail, but it was almost too late. Under the pressure of the wind, the Viking vessel heeled so far that the starboard gunnel was shipping water. The big sail wouldn't come down; the ship lay groaning on its side. Winds were shoving the sail back up the mast. Crewmembers solved the problem by wrestling the sail down by hand.

Dawn came with the waves growing in height, but the wind had abated. The crew hoisted the reefed sail.

The *Hjemkomst* flew along. Overrunning one big wave, her hull went airborne. She slammed down with a shock—and a cracking noise. Water gurgled in the bilge.

Their ship had a fourteen-foot-long crack in one plank.

They bailed, stuffed the crack and sailed on. Now the winds were giving them a real ride; the long, straight hull was showing them its Viking heritage, flying over the waves.

The hull flexed and bent, snaking its way through the waves—the way the ancient shipwrights had designed this vessel. It went so fast that waves wrapped around the aft section of the vessel, dousing the helmsman.

There was not a dry place on deck. Their food began to mold, their drinking water tasted of sea salt.

As she passed England and entered the North Sea, the homecoming ship seemed to move faster as her destination neared.

On the 19th of July, after 34 days at sea, the *Hjemkomst* arrived in Norway.

······················· ※ ·····················

When the *Hjemkomst* entered Bergen Harbor, 600 vessels came out to greet her. Drummer boys began drum rolls as each of the crew disembarked to stand on Norwegian soil. A band played both the American and the Norwegian anthems. Flags flying, the people of Norway welcomed the Viking ship as if it were a long-lost relative returning to their home shores.

In midst of the festivities, someone asked for a moment of silence for Bob Asp, the man whose ghost seemed to have ridden on the ship. Heads bowed, they remembered him with warmth in their hearts.

The Hjemkomst began her tour of her beloved land. Cheers and greetings came from shore,

King Olaf, of Norway, came in his own ship to see the Viking vessel. With gratitude, the crew went on board the king's yacht to hear his congratulations. But they made a startling discovery. Looking back at their boat, they saw that the *Hjemkomst* was riding so low in the water that even her floorboards were floating. The crack had opened up

As the King watched and waved, the crew dashed back to their ship and began bailing.

The final part of their homecoming took them to Oslo. Flags flying, a flotilla of boats and ships came out to greet them. Thousands of well-wishers crowded the shore. They docked their ship at the Pier of Honor, reserved for the ships of the king and other dignitaries.

It was a huge welcome to the first Americans to cross the Atlantic in a Viking vessel. There were tears in the eyes of the crew members as they, and their homecoming ship, reached the end of their destination.

They were at last home. ☀

3

Courage of the sole survivor

★ ★ ★

He stayed alive on an ice-coated raft

HER STARBOARD SIDE LASHED by mounting waves, the *S.S. Daniel J. Morrell* clawed northward. It was Nov. 28, 1966, and a fall blizzard had overtaken Lake Huron. As the night deepened, the ore boat began to blow around, pitching and rolling in 25-foot high seas.

Launched in 1906 and rated at 7,763 gross tons, the *Morrell* was 600 feet long, 60 feet wide and drew 27 feet. She was a tough ship. The *Morrell* had been caught in the 1958 Lake Superior storm that had sunk another ore vessel, the *Bradley*. Despite 100 mile-per-hour winds and high seas, the *Morrell* had come through unscathed.

By 2 a.m., she had fought her way off the thumb of Michigan's "mitten," known as the graveyard for ships. The seas were confused, running both from the north-northeast and the north-northwest. They swept her length; she took green water over her bow.

In his forward quarters, able-bodied seaman Dennis Hale was asleep. The 26-year-old, 250-pound Hale woke up when books fell off his bookshelf with a loud bang.

Dennis sat up and tried to click on his bunk light. The bulb stayed dark.

When the emergency bell split the night to sound the general alarm, Dennis grabbed a life jacket and rushed on deck. Gusts of wind hit him; he staggered to stand upright. Standing barefoot and ankle deep in icy slush, clad only in his life jacket and undershorts, he shivered as he peered down the spar deck. Something was wrong with the boat.

In the center, the steel deck was grinding up and down. Sparks flew from the twisting metal; steam billowed out.

Suddenly, the midsection reared high in the air. The boat was breaking apart.

Dennis dashed back to his cabin to find more clothing, but in the darkness, he could only grab his wool pea coat. He threw that on over his lifejacket and hurried back to the deck. He felt the snow on his face, the frigid wind on his naked legs and the ice under his bare toes.

Shivering, he climbed aboard the pontoon life raft, lashed atop a hatch behind the pilothouse. A last-ditch survival unit with no weather protection for the crew, the raft was constructed of two eight-foot-long steel pontoons, topped with a flat decking of wooden planks. In the center was a compartment with emergency signaling gear. The raft was too heavy to pick up and throw overboard; it could only be launched if the bow section sank and the raft floated off.

The ship had lifeboats, but these were located in the aft section— unreachable to Dennis and his crewmates over the cracking hull. Some crew were already sitting in the raft; some stood alongside. One man lashed himself to the raft.

Everyone remained calm. They talked among themselves, but they knew they were in trouble. They could not send a Mayday. The power cables, running from the engine room in the stern to the forward section, had snapped with the breakup of the hull.

Dennis tried to mooch a cigarette from a buddy. He didn't have any luck.

.... ❈ ....

Dennis saw the one-inch thick steel deck tear in half, from one side to another. The gap widened; the aft section separated from the hull. Lights burned inside the separated hull; it glowed an eerie yellow. Puffs of smoke erupted. Engine still running, propeller churning, the cavernous aft section charged forward. It headed straight toward them.

Dennis grabbed a handhold on the raft. As the aft hull section came nearer, he closed his eyes.

The next thing he recalled was struggling beneath icy waters. He fought his way to the surface. Atop the waves, the pontoon raft's automatic emergency light beckoned to him in the darkness. He had survived a 50-foot fall into heavy seas.

Exhausted and shivering, he pulled himself aboard the life raft, where he found deckhands Arthur Sojek, 33, and John Cleary, Jr., 20. Minutes later, they helped pull wheelman Charles Fossbender from the icy waters.

Only four men had survived the fall and made it to raft. They scanned the seas and yelled. No survivors answered. In the storage compartment, they found flares, a flare gun, and a flashlight. They fired off some flares to signal any ships in the area. None responded.

Minutes later, Charles Fossbender waved the flashlight back and forth, signaling what appeared to be a nearby ship.

Dennis shielded his eyes in the spray. He shook his head.

It was not a ship to rescue them. In the storm, Fossbender had mistaken the _Morrell's_ ghostly stern, still lighted and under power, sailing away.

.... ❋ ....

Exposed to the driving winds and freezing spray, the survivors huddled on the platform over the two pontoons. None were dressed much better than Dennis. Only Charles Fossbender, who had been on watch, was fully clothed.

By dawn, John Cleary and Art Stojek were dead. Only Dennis and Fossbender remained alive. Dennis lay on his left side, his head cradled under one arm, near the collapsed storage compartment. Fossbender was behind him, facing away, curled with his legs up. Both men shivered uncontrollably.

At about 2 p.m., Fossbender raised himself. "I can see land."

"How far away is it?"

"Quite a distance." Two hours later, Fossbender was dead.

Dennis was alone on a frozen raft, surrounded by his dead friends. Cleary and Stojek died around 0600 hours and Fossbender died at about 1600 hours. The first two men had endured about six hours of exposure; the third man, about 16 hours.

Dennis attempted to move parts of his body to keep up circulation. He put his fingers in his mouth so they would not freeze. He didn't urinate for fear that the warmth he had in his groin would escape and he'd die. By his own estimate, he held his urine for over 24 hours to save his internal body heat.

Several hundred feet from shore, the raft ran aground on rocks. Dennis could see lights from a farmhouse. To get help, he fired several flares, holding the broken flare gun together with his bare hands. No one saw his signals. He yelled when he heard the sounds of people. No one answered.

He tried to move from the raft but he was paralyzed by the cold. His unused muscles knotted with cramps. In pain, he could only watch.

He couldn't give up hope. If he remained where he was, someone would see the raft. They'd come out to rescue him. Somebody somewhere would notice that the *Morrell* was missing, and they'd send a search party.

He nursed himself through the long day with hopes. By nightfall, the wind arose again and cold descended on his numbed body. Breakers rolled over the raft. Dennis drifted in and out of sleep. Ice coated him.

The next morning, right after dawn, he awoke with a start. He saw the farmhouse lights come on. He yelled and yelled again for help, but no one answered.

It began to snow.

····················· ❀ ·····················

By afternoon, thirst ravaged him. Earlier, he had been able to lick a few drops of lake water off the lanyard of his flare gun, but that was gone now. Ice had formed on his pea coat. Painfully, he moved his head about, ready to suck the ice on his coat when he saw something that stopped him.

Floating above the raft and looking down on him was a man dressed all in white. He had a white mustache and white hair, with translucent, bluish skin. His eyes burned with intensity.

"Don't eat the ice off your pea coat," he commanded in a loud voice. He vanished as mysteriously as he had arrived.

Dennis laid his head back down on the raft, still thirsty. Wind howled across the wave crests, sweeping across his ice-coated body. He lost track of time.

After a while, he felt himself floating, moving upward, as if a force had come up behind him and was sucking him away from the raft. As he rose higher and higher, he felt his pain and the cold receding.

He headed toward a white light, as if at the end of a tunnel. When he emerged, he saw a green, grassy field, well cut, with a little depression, and a bridge going across it.

A man dressed in white stood waiting. He took Dennis's hands in his and said, "Let us see what you have learned."

Dennis's whole life flashed before him as he answered the man's questions. When Dennis finished, the man released the sailor's hands and told him he could pass over.

On the bridge's other side, his mother appeared. He recognized her only from pictures. She told him how glad she was to see him at last. Long-dead loved ones and relatives gathered around.

He descended into a mist until he came to the bow of the *Morrell*, lying in a valley. Aboard were all his old shipmates. They hugged and clapped him on the back.

Out of the mist glided the stern section of the *Morrell*. It joined up with the forward section almost seamlessly. Dennis and his shipmates rushed to it and clambered down below, where they found the rest of the crew at work. They talked about how glad they were to be together again.

The third engineer, George Dahl, came up a ladder, and stared at Dennis. "What are you doing here?" he asked. "It's not your time." All conversation stopped.

Someone said, "You've got to go back," and Dennis was lifted into the whirlwind.

He was back on the raft, all alone. His thirst had returned. He began to bite at ice when the man in white again appeared overhead. He shook a finger at Dennis. "I told you not to eat the ice off your pea coat," he warned. "It'll lower your body temperature and you'll die."

Dennis stopped eating ice.

.... ❈ ....

In the offices of the Bethlehem Steel fleet, the chief dispatcher was worried. The reporting station at the locks at Sault Ste. Marie had not reported the *Morrell's* arrival, nor that of the *Townsend*, also out in the gale. On Wednesday morning, he called the Coast Guard, who located the *Townsend* anchored in the St. Mary's river.

But where was the *Morrell*?

At 1:12 p.m. Wednesday, they sighted a body at Harbor Beach. When the Coast Guard recovered it, they saw the man wore a life jacket with the *Morrell's* name on it. The Coast Guard broadcast an alert. An hour later, a freighter saw wreckage about four miles north-northeast of Harbor Beach. The freighter picked up ring buoys and an oil can from the *Morrell*. At 2 p.m., the crew recovered three bodies.

They searched the snow-covered shoreline. Late in the afternoon, a helicopter crew saw a life raft bobbing near the shore. On it appeared to be four dead men, encased in ice.

One of them raised his hand, waving feebly.

The helicopter landed on its pontoons in the shallow, choppy water. Crewmen splashed out, wading toward the raft. They had to roll the half-frozen man off.

At Harbor Beach, an ambulance rushed Dennis to the hospital. He had lost some skin from his hands and there was frostbite on his left foot. His skin hadn't turned black, but his body temperature hovered at 94 degrees, dangerously below normal. They packed anything that would hold warm water around his body to raise his temperature.

Out on Huron, boats crisscrossed the lake to fish out bodies. Of the *Morrell's* 29-man crew, they recovered only twenty frozen corpses. Eight men are still missing.

Only one man had returned alive.

.... ❋ ....

When I met him at the Minnesota State Historical Society's building in Saint Paul, Dennis had a limp and moved down the stairs hesitantly. A big man well over six feet, he was in his 60s, with silver hair.

Dennis lost 50 pounds and suffered damage to his left arm. His frostbitten feet were his biggest problem, and, over a period of years, he had one operation on the right foot and ten on the left.

When he related his feat of holding his urine for 24 hours to a crusty hospital nurse, she cut him off short: "Yeah, what if that had frozen inside you?" Dennis retells that story with a smile. He did not have an answer.

After decades of silence, he told me that only in recent years has he been able to talk about "Doc," the man in white that visited him when he was on the raft, or his remarkable out-of-body experiences. The tragedy had traumatized him into silence.

On Death Certificates, Dennis found out that his three crewmates' cause of death was drowning. Exposure was " an antecedent cause." That surprised him. But he remembered that Charlie Fossbinder had complained that his lungs were filling up from the foam and the spray. The men were all believed to be conscious until shortly before death. Dennis later learned that although Charlie Fossbender never complained, his chest had been crushed. Both of his shoulders were broken.

As I walked from the lecture hall, I realized that Dennis had given sailors a special gift: resilience. One should never give up, no matter how grim the situation—even if you are frozen to the bottom of an open life raft in stormy seas.

All of us can survive far longer and far better than anyone had ever thought possible.

He had. ☸

4

Warriors of the storm

✩✩✩

You have to go out—
You don't have to come back

THE WIND WAS GUSTING TO 30 KNOTS, packing Superior's white-caps close together. Carefully monitoring the depth sounder's readings, I was following the bottom's contours and steering the 36-foot catamaran close to shore. By maintaining a 30-foot depth, I would have ample water under our keel.

I was taking no chances: Today we were sailing along the Shipwreck Coast—the "graveyard of the Great Lakes."

The coastal area was mostly desolate sand dunes and scrub pines. Coming into view, I saw what appeared to be a weather-beaten frame structure, fallen down in places. The Vermilion Point Station was once the most isolated lifesaving station on Lake Superior. Opened in 1876, the crews of the United States Life-Saving Service on Lake Superior were genuine folk heroes known as the Warriors of the Storm.

Their unofficial motto: You have to go out. You don't have to come back.

The Life Saver's surfboat was a wooden 25-foot rowing vessel, light-weight for its size at 700 to 1,000 pounds. Crews in harnesses could haul it in a trailer to the water's edge near a wreck. The boat was self-bailing and self-righting; water that came in would run out, and, if overturned, the boat would right itself. The craft was undecked and open; waves could sweep over the crew. The surf men sat two abreast, in three pairs, each manning an oar, so that six oars powered a surfboat.

The Captain was in the stern using an extra-long oar trailing behind to steer. An oar was better than a tiller since it gave more control in extreme conditions

The Warriors lived a Spartan life in a lifesaving station on duty 24 hours a day. Scanning the waves, a lookout always was on watch in an open lookout tower He had to ring a bell every hour to prove that he was still awake. The lookout posts were without seats, so he could stand but not sit. At night, beach patrols with lanterns in hand walked along the shore, searching for a vessel being overwhelmed by a storm, a wreck coming ashore, or even debris or bodies washed up by the waves.

They had to be expert sailors and boatmen, couldn't be younger than 18 years of age nor older than 45; couldn't weigh less than 135 pounds or over 205, and, had to be expert swimmers. Their pay was $65 a month; the Station Keeper got $10 more.

New recruits were warned to beware the ghost of Three-Fingered Riley, a seaman washed ashore during a winter storm. When they tried to chop the corpse's hand out of the ice, they slipped—and cut off two of Riley's fingers. According to legend, he's still looking for his missing fingers. So, beware of Riley on that cold, stormy night's patrol.

Some of their sea rescues seem almost incredible:

*A northwest gale August 26, 1896, caught the 177-foot three-masted schooner *Phineas S. Marsh* off the Shipwreck Coast's Crisp Point. Leaking in the heavy seas, she tried to make it into the safety of Whitefish Point. Seas boarded her decks; water rose in the bilges. When the Crisp Point Station lifesavers saw the *Marsh's* distress flare, they launched their lifeboat through the heavy surf. It took them two-and-a-half hours to row off the shore in high waves, but as they neared the doomed schooner, the *Marsh* rolled to port, then sank to the bottom, only 22 feet below. Waves washed two of the crew and a cook overboard; the rest of the crew scrambled up the masts and rigging, which heeled at an angle to one side. The lifeboat maneuvered under the canted mast and swaying rigging to haul the drowning cook out of the water. As the Life-Savers backed their oars, several of the *Marsh's* crew in the rigging dropped into the lifeboat, injuring one of the Life Savers. The lifeboat pulled away from the wreck and landed three survivors on the beach. They fought their way back to the wreck in two more trips to rescue the rest of the crew. They saved everyone.

*Late in the shipping season, the Warriors had to face not only stormy seas but also bitter cold and snow. On November 15, 1887, a northern gale caught the *Starrucca*, a 218-foot wooden steamer, as she headed upbound for Duluth, Minnesota. About 10 miles east of Grand Marais, Michigan, during snow squalls and heavy waves, she drove onto a sandbar about a half-mile offshore. The Deer Park Life Savers launched their surfboat and rowed 12 miles to the stricken *Starrucca*. When they reached her at about 5 p.m., the *Starrucca* captain decided he'd stay aboard until the seas became more moderate; then he'd try to save his vessel. The Life Savers rowed back to the beach and set up camp to keep watch on the grounded vessel.

But the storm got worse; breakers slammed over the vessel's cabins. At midnight, the captain signaled for help and the Life Savers fought their way from the storm-scoured shore. Freezing spray inundated them; waves swept on board. They made three trips to haul the crew back to land. When they finished, the Life-Savers were frostbitten, half frozen and exhausted. Inches of ice coated their clothing, their equipment and their surfboat.

*Late in October 1887, the *Alva Bradley*, a 189-foot wooden schooner, ran aground in gale-force winds and thick snow near Marquette, Michigan. Seas twenty feet high overran her deck and tore away her yawl boat; ice coated her railings, decks, rigging and lower masts. Pounded against rocks by heavy waves, she was in danger of breaking up. The Portage Lake Life Saving Station, near the Portage Lake Ship Canal, heard the call for help later in the afternoon. But the Life-Savers were 130 miles from the wreck site.

In the storm, Capt. Ocha and his crew of eight rowed their boat to Houghton, Michigan. They lashed it on a flatcar behind a locomotive which roared through the snow-covered countryside. Later that night, when the train arrived at Marquette, Michigan, the Life-Savers unloaded their boat and equipment onto wagons and dragged them to the surf's edge. At 1 a.m., they climbed in their boat and tied it behind the tugboat, *A.C. Adams*, to give them a tow into the blustering lake. It was the worst storm of the season.

In their open surfboat, the Life-Savers felt the full force of the gale.

Spray coated them, their boat, and their oars turned to ice When it was time to row to the stricken vessel, where the tugboat could not go, they cut the ice-frozen tow line and rowed in the darkness toward the stranded schooner's anchor light. An hour later, the Life-Savers were alongside the schooner; the *Bradley's* crew crawled aboard. When they rowed back to the rendezvous point, the tugboat *A. C. Adams* had departed because of a mix-up in signals. Alone on the lake, the Life-Savers began to row to Marquette.

Lying in the surfboat's bottom and shivering in the icy water, the *Bradley's* sailors begged to return to their stricken schooner. The surfboat returned to the *Bradley* at about 4 a.m. and her crewmen went aboard to warm up. At dawn, when the *Bradley* was in danger of breaking up, her crew and the Life Savers scrambled back onboard the icy surfboat.

Capt. Ocha headed toward a bonfire that townspeople had built on the beach as an all-night vigil. With great skill, he ran the dangerous breakers and put his surfboat on shore. The *Bradley's* crew members were carried to the fire, warmed and fed, and later taken through the woods to a waiting train. The Life-Savers again launched their boat into the surf and rowed out to the rescue tugboat, which had returned at daylight. They took up the towline; the tug shouldered its way through the storm to Marquette. When the Life Savers reached the docks, townspeople had to chop them from their ice-crusted boat. Their frozen clothing had to be cut away to let them out.

*In September 1899, the Life Saving Station at Marquette, Michigan, came up with an innovation: they added a motor to their lifeboat. By modern standards, their power plant was primitive, cranky, and underpowered. Still, it gave the Life Savers more range and the ability to slug it out longer to rescue shipwreck crews.

An ultimate survival test for their power lifeboat came on December 7, 1927, when the *Altadoc*, 365 feet long and upbound to Fort William, lost her steering gear in heavy seas. Helpless in the waves churned by 70-mile-an-hour gusts and blinded by heavy snow, she and her crew of 25 drove hard ashore on the Keweenaw Point's rocks.

At Eagle Harbor, over 23 miles away, the Life Saving Station heard the stricken vessel's emergency radio transmissions and contacted their Boatswain, Anthony F. Glaza, who had been on liberty in Hancock,

Michigan. Snow clogged the roads. When Glaza started back in the blizzard, he traveled first by streetcar, then by county snowplow and then by riding in a horse-drawn sleigh. He walked the last six miles; by midnight, he was at his station.

But the harbor was jammed with ice. Because his boat could not get out, Glaza loaded his motorized surfboat on a sleigh and hired a team of horses to pull the boat around the bay. He and his crew wrestled their boat across the packed ice field until they could splash it into the waves. That took about five hours.

They plunged through heavy seas for two-and-a-half hours until their boat came alongside the wrecked freighter. Two of the Life-Saving crew volunteered to go aboard to make room in the lifeboat. Fourteen of the ship's crew made their way down into the ice-coated surfboat. Glaza turned his helm for Copper Harbor; at 3 p.m., the LifeSavers put the *Altadoc* crew on shore. Then they fought their way back to pick up the rest of the men.

Returning to Copper Harbor at 6:30 that evening, the motorized surfboat became iced in. To free it, the Life-Savers rocked the boat in the inch-and-a-half thick ice. Water sloshed onto the engine; it stopped. They were powerless and stranded in a field of ice.

From the distance, a searchlight shone: It was the Coast Guard cutter *Crawford*, which had fought its way across Superior despite 27 degrees-below-zero cold. The cutter broke a path through the ice to the surfboat and took the Life Savers and the *Altadoc* crew on board.

The next morning, the *Crawford* left for Eagle Harbor, towing the surfboat behind. Entering the harbor, the cutter began to maneuver through the thick ice, but damaged both propellers. The Life Savers dropped onto the ice and manhandled their surfboat across the frozen surface back to their station.

They found four planks cracked and the boat's sides cut by the ice, but the gallant little boat had won. Not a single man was lost to Superior.

As I sailed past the remains of the old Life Saving station, I took off my cap in silent tribute. The old Warriors of the Storm were incredible mariners with enormous courage and great resourcefulness. ❈

5

Ten feet across the Pacific

★ ★ ★

Gary Spiess sails the world's largest ocean

ON THE NINTH DAY OF THE VOYAGE, big rollers started to form. It was the Pacific Ocean's convergence zone, where a cold current that flows from Alaska meets the warm central current. One set of waves was running 8 to 12 feet; the other sets ran at over 8 feet. Worse yet, the wave trains were colliding.

A splash of spray hit Gerry Spiess in the face—the water was cold.

Slamming his hatch shut, Gerry slumped back into his cabin and crawled into the warmth of his sleeping bag. He was thankful that he had decided earlier to take down all sails and run under bare poles—a standard procedure for rough weather.

Hawaii was over 1,800 miles away—and looking distant.

.... ❁ ....

There was a heavy thump. Sheets of water poured through the closed hatch. Gerry looked up to see a small Niagara flooding inside the cabin.

A wave had overrun *Yankee Girl*. It turned the little sloop into a submarine, with only her mast sticking out. The water pressure blasted through the sliding hatch closure.

She fought her way free of the wave, but the steep seas were so bad that even running under bare poles wasn't working. She couldn't take any more water over her transom.

Gerry threw back the hatch and climbed onto the wet deck. In the moonlight, he saw a huge wave roaring toward him. He didn't have time to duck back into the cockpit, so he slammed shut the open hatch below him. He lunged forward on the cabin top to the mast.

The wave roared over the transom. With Gerry atop the deck, *Yankee Girl* careened to one side.

She paused a moment, then righted herself.

When the wave passed, Gerry began working on the sails. With one hand clamped on the mast, he wedged a foot on the starboard shroud and chain plate and crouched down. From this position, he reached forward to unleash the jib, secured under shock chord along the bow's starboard side. Gerry hanked the sail onto the forestay; tied the jib halyard to the sail and crossed the jib sheet to the opposite side. He unleashed the mainsail from alongside the boom.

Gerry tumbled back into the cockpit and hoisted the reefed main and the jib, throwing the tiller to the opposite side. *Yankee Girl* pointed her bow into the wind and waves.

Heaving to was astonishing and immediate, as if the ocean had calmed. *Yankee Girl* moved forward, then fell off a little, then resumed her motion ahead. Instead of being bashed in her broad, flat transom by waves, her bow speared into them and shoved them to one side. With her sails up, she had balance, poise and direction.

Gerry dogged down the hatch and relaxed as much as he could. He had done all he could for her. Now she'd have to look after him.

··················· ❁ ···················

By dawn, the motion of *Yankee Girl* had changed. The sun was high, but the Pacific spread lumpy and empty to every horizon. *Yankee Girl's* sails were beginning to slat and flutter. They were becalmed.

Gerry checked his outboard. Waves battered it all night long: he'd heard it shudder and bang. He wondered if it'd been torn off.

But his engine was still on its motor mount. It was a two-cycle out-board Evinrude. He'd always had great luck with the two-cycles. On his stormy North Atlantic crossing, waves had beaten and doused his elderly 4-hp. outboard. Behind him was a brand new 4.5-hp. engine.

These engines always fire up, Gerry thought. He pulled the starting cord through to get the gas up.

Then he yanked another time—hard.

Nothing happened.

The outboard would not start. It would spin through, but not catch and fire up.

He raised the throttle arm and peered beneath. The engine had a shut-off or kill button at the end of the throttle arm. If you pushed the button, the engine stopped. The waves had shorted out the kill switch.

With a needle-nose pliers from his repair kit, he snipped its wires. This bypassed the problem. He crossed his fingers and hauled hard on the start-er cord. With a chuff of smoke, the little two-stroke started up and soon settled into a raspy idle.

He ran his engine at a fast idle, giving him a cruising speed of around 2.2 knots (2.53 mph). For the next six days, *Yankee Girl* motored nonstop day and night toward Hawaii. To refuel, he'd unscrew the filler top of his six-gallon main gas tank inside the cabin, pour in gas from one of many gas cans he carried in the bilge, screw back the top, and, continued cruis-ing. He did not stop his engine to refuel.

He stopped it to change the engine's single spark plug—cheap insur-ance, he figured.

Slow, but consistent running was part of his crossing strategy. It took patience but gave him great gas mileage since the two cycle single-cylin-der engine only used a fraction of a gallon per hour. That meant one gallon of pre-mixed gas and oil would last over seven hours. A 24-hour day's run would consume only 3.5 gallons. He carried 54 gallons of pre-mixed gas on board, most of it in the bilges, down low for ballast.

At low speeds, *Yankee Girl's* cruising was effortless, but noisy. When he was piloting the boat, he sat in the aft bunk, with his head near the tran-som and the purring outboard, or, when he slept, his head was just a few feet from the engine.

He found he couldn't get away from the outboard's noise.

His engine speeded up. Odd, Gerry thought. He looked up to see his sails starting to draw.

It was the third stage of his trip to Hawaii and the one he looked for-ward to the most. He shut down the outboard by choking it off and let the trade winds carry him to the islands. His boat was a wind ship again.

Soaring along in the trades was a wonderful feeling. *Yankee Girl* bowled along on a peaceful, rolling sea. The Pacific was living up to its legends.

Gerry hoisted his twin jibs, each 39-square foot, a little bigger than a beach towel. He poled them out to resemble two odd-shaped triangles. By sheeting each jib, he could control the sails from the safety of his cockpit.

Yankee Girl steered herself in the trade winds. With the twin jibs pulling her along like small ponies, her daily run increased. Some days, she'd do 85 nautical miles; some days, 95.

Gerry relaxed in the open cockpit, enjoying his fine pocket cruiser in the warm trade winds and bright sunshine. This was the South Pacific, and, as he peered into the water, he saw that its color had changed to a deep indigo blue. He reached over and cupped a handful just to admire its beauty.

For his navigation, he had on board two Davis plastic sextants. This included a sextant he bought for $30, and, had used to cross the Atlantic. He used the $30 one because he liked it so much.

When he neared the Hawaiian Islands, he turned on his transistor radio and listened to a broadcast from a Hawaiian station. He had an aircraft radio on board, and he could hear pilots somewhere in the skies checking with air controllers to prepare for landing.

As one flight high in the sky came overhead, Gerry called to it via his aircraft radio. He told them where he was and gave them his GPS coordinates, but after several tries, the pilots could not make him out in the waves below. Gerry watched their contrails etch white against the blue sky.

The jet would land in Honolulu in 40 minutes. He'd be there in about five days.

.... ✻ ....

Off in the distance, the islands of Hawaii rose to greet him, first the Big Island, Maui, and then Molokai. Blue peaks emerged out of a light hazing of mist.

It was his first sighted landfall in 2,500 miles, and, the islands were right where his plastic sextant told him they'd be. Gerry steered around the northern edge of Molokai. He looked for a small beach with a sand bottom and protection from the trade winds.

It was late afternoon when he dropped his anchor. He opened the hatch wide so he could enjoy the Hawaiian breezes; *Yankee Girl* bobbed in the blue waters. From the bow area, he brought up empty gas cans, which he filled with seawater, so he'd have the right trim. Since *Yankee Girl* did not have any permanent ballast, but relied upon stores for weight below, he had to maintain the right load in the bilges.

Checking his main gas tank, he figured he'd have enough gas left to make it to Honolulu. No need to top it up: he'd do a lot of sailing in the trade winds. He'd only need to run his engine for maneuvering.

Tropical breezes wafted over him. For supper, Gerry treated himself to his favorite meal, a can of Dinty Moore beef stew. Exhausted, he fell asleep. It was a good night's sleep in the great island's shadow, bobbing in protected blue waters.

Tomorrow would be the homecoming.

.... ❈ ....

The media had been out in chartered boats to film *Yankee Girl's* arrival but now were back, looking somewhat green.

"God that was rough," one of them said.

It had been a wild ride. The Kaiwi Channel lies between the islands of Molokai and Oahu and funnels both trade winds and currents into fast-moving, high waves. Even many local sailors don't venture out into the rough Kaiwi Channel.

But it was a sleigh ride for Gerry heading past Diamond Head. Speeding along on one jib, he sat on the starboard side of the cockpit, bracing himself in the rollers, and waving cheerfully to members of the press.

In the Waikiki Yacht Club bar, I waited. I kept hearing Gerry's voice on the club's tinny VHF radio. *Yankee Girl* had arrived outside the break-waters. He seemed impatient to come in.

I knew why. He was waiting for someone to guide him into the harbor, and, that someone was sitting at a table in front of me.

The captain was playing cards. He explained, "I need to finish this hand."

These were the islands. Matters were done on island time. Minutes later, the card game ended.

"Let's go," he said. We walked along the Ali Wai small boat harbor quay and boarded his trawler.

Underway, it was easy to figure out where *Yankee Girl* was located. She was surrounded by a small squadron of boats. Gerry was standing in the cockpit, rolling back and forth in their wake.

From the trawler's bridge, I called down to Gerry and then waved. Gerry seemed to squint but did not recognize me. I tried the VHF radio but got no response.

I shouted, "Follow us."

Gerry began following the trawler into the harbor. He was escorted by some inquisitive boats that formed an informal parade. He tied up in the guest of honor berth at the club, right in front of the open-air restaurant. The word had spread around the island. People gathered to see the remarkable little boat and its builder-skipper.

After his long sea voyage, Gerry had to be helped from the boat. He was supported on both sides by his wife, Sally, and, his dad, Lou.

"Marlin," Gerry said, after staring at me. "You made it."

I marveled at how well he looked—sun tanned and healthy, with a dark beard. Despite being in his boat for over a month, he appeared nattily dressed in clean, pressed clothing, just as if he had just stepped from one of the beautiful Honolulu hotels.

Gerry's knack for detail was paying off: he had packed a plastic canister with clean, fresh clothes just for this occasion. He put them on this morning.

.... ※ ....

After Honolulu, Gerry headed southwest to Fanning Island, a tiny atoll. From there, he sailed to American Samoa and Fiji. He ended the voyage with a hero's welcome in Sydney, Australia. It was a crossing for the record books: *Yankee Girl* was the smallest vessel to cross the South Pacific.

The voyage from Long Beach, California, to Honolulu, Hawaii, had had taken 34 days. Under all conditions including calms and storms, *Yankee Girl* sailed 2,200 nautical miles (2,539 statute) and averaged 65 nautical miles a day (74.75 statute). This is an extraordinary performance for a solo vessel.

Gerry estimated, "I was asleep a third of the time."

Yankee Girl kept getting better. As he got further in the South Pacific's trade winds, *Yankee Girl* often would reel off 100 nautical miles a day. Best day ever was 120 nautical miles in a 24-hour run during the last miles of her trans-Pacific crossing.

Yankee Girl was a monumental boat on a 9-foot 9-inch waterline. As a bare hull, she tipped the scales at less than 440 pounds. With her running gear, she weighed 750 pounds; loaded up with food and supplies to her cabin rooftop, she weighed a whopping 2,200 pounds. Gerry joked, "I had to eat my way in."

Gerry designed *Yankee Girl* to be an all-weather slugger, not just a fair wind sailor. He felt that a sailor needs protection from the elements. ("You don't go out there to rough it; you go out there to smooth it.")

Long before he took her to the ocean, Gerry had spent a lot of time aboard his boat, sleeping, eating and sailing. He told me, you never want to go to sea in a new boat, only an "old boat."

Gerry said that a voyage wasn't "… a series of chance events, a time when I'd be cast adrift in a universe of incalculable dimensions. Instead, I surrounded myself with details, all of which could be isolated, analyzed, and, acted upon. I meant to be in control at all times."

His strategy was to keep moving at all times. If there was no wind, he would run his two-cycle engine at a fast idle. On flat water, with no head-wind, this would give him a speed of about 2.2 knots–2.53 statute miles per hour. Under engine power, *Yankee Girl* covered 50 nautical miles per day, and, when he hit the Pacific current, which gave him a boost of a fraction of a knot, his total day's run could hit 60 nautical miles. His speed exceeded what the *Mayflower* could average on a day's run. The Pilgrim's 100-foot ship averaged about 2 nautical miles per hour and sailed only 48 nautical miles per day.

Gerry joked with dockside power boaters. With their hundreds and sometimes thousands of horsepower, they were not impressed with Gerry's outboard.

"How much range do you get?" Gerry'd ask.

They'd reply that they averaged a 200- to 350-mile range.

Gerry would tell them that *Yankee Girl* had almost a thousand-mile range.

He did the math for them. *Yankee Girl* carried 54 gallons of pre-mix and he'd get 17 statute miles to a gallon. That would give him a range of 918 miles. His 4.5-hp. outboard could push the boat faster than her usual fast-idle cruising speed of 2 ½ miles per hour, but that was not part of his plan. He did not want to go fast, only far.

For clothing, he carried 35 pairs of shorts and T-shirts, 35 pairs of socks, 10 pairs of pants, 28 long-sleeved shirts, a down jacket, 5 sweaters, and 2 suits of foul weather gear, plus rubber gloves (3 pairs), and wool gloves (1) and 5 caps. He had learned he could get a lot of clothing into a plastic jug if he wrapped the clothing tightly. Because he had no way to wash the salt from the garments, much less dry them, he'd wear each item only once, and throw it overboard. It would dissolve in the sea.

Despite his mastery of details, Gerry once nearly ran out of gas. It happened at the time I came out to meet him in the trawler. Though he had several gallons of gas left, he had not refilled his main tank when he left his overnight Molokai anchorage because he figured he had enough gas to maneuver.

He had to motor to get out of his anchorage, and, nearing Oahu, had to run his engine to get past the lee of Diamond Head. When he got into the channel, he turned off his engine and had a windy sleigh ride into Honolulu. Nearing the Ali Wai small boat harbor, he had to fire up his outboard to maneuver when boats surrounded him. When he tied up in the guest of honor space in front of the yacht club, he was running on fumes. He told me later that it would have been embarrassing for him to run out of gas and be towed the final few yards to his destination.

After he arrived at Sydney, Australia, to a hero's welcome, Gerry returned to his native Minnesota. He donated *Yankee Girl* to the Minnesota Historical Society, where she is now a part of the society's historical treasures. Gerry visited her from time to time and, he told me he sometimes wishes he had "his little girl" back.

Gerry had enormous pride in her: She was his creation. He had designed and built her. He sailed her across the North Atlantic and the South Pacific, both to new world records and maritime acclaim. What she and her sailor did ranks among the world's greatest seafaring accomplishments. Her adventures continue to fire the imaginations of mariners everywhere.

Throughout his work, Gerry had a special perspective: After you have done everything you can do, and thought everything through, then one of two things can happen: You can succeed, or, you can have a wonderful time trying. ☀

6

The lost mariners

*Divers find a sunken ship
and its missing crew*

PERSISTENCE WAS PUNCHING THROUGH THE WAVES, spray splashing from her bow. We were nearing the north shore's Castle Danger and were taking a pounding–more than I wanted for my home-built 20-foot sloop. I felt a raw breath on my right cheek. As I turned my face and one ear to figure out its direction; the breeze seemed to intensify.

It was an ancient wind sailor's trick: use your face, then your ear, then your ear hairs to figure out what direction the wind is coming from. No complicated electronics.

But the news was not good.

Out of the mist roared a howling gale. I was on a lee shore and I could see the outline of reefs, framed in white–the surf.

I threw the tiller over, but the wind began to lever the mast down into the water. No doubt about it: I was caught in a northeaster.

Whump! The breakers hit the wooden hull. Spurts of chill water gushed into the cockpit. I had a foreboding and glanced to starboard. The rocks had grown.

We were being swept too close. I worked the tiller, and we began to claw away, heading toward safe open water. The mist was thickening; another storm seemed to brew.

As I entered Two Harbors' misty entryway, I could breathe easier. I tied *Persistence* to a rusty barge, near an old tugboat. I was safe, for a little while. And home for the night.

.... ❋ ....

Night fell. The fog blurred the lights on the nearby ore docks. The waterfront was lonely, primitive and downright strange. Time to move out. I pulled on my heavy sailing sweater and my yachting parka. I closed my hatch.

Picking my way across the barge, I clambered onto a wet dock. It was an uphill walk through the pine-filled woods but soon the mining company's small security shack loomed in front of me. Yellow light flooded out of the windows.

I tapped the window and Bill Burke motioned me to the side door.

"I heard you were back on the dock." He smiled.

Heh. Heh. News had passed on the waterfront that the lone sailor trying to sail to Canada, didn't make it. Again.

He poured a cup of black coffee. As I sipped the bitter brew, I began to warm up in the guardhouse. Superior could be brisk, even in July, if you live onboard a small unheated craft.

Bill was a fellow SCUBA diver and had an intense interest in what lay below Superior's surface. He had been on a few shipwrecks and had sea stories to tell. I sat back with my coffee mug and listened.

"Before I had a back injury, I used to do a lot of scuba diving up here," Bill began. "In fact, I was among the first to explore the Canadian steamer, the *Emperor.* She struck Canoe Rocks off Isle Royale in 1947 and still lies in 150 feet of water, with her stern sticking out over a deep cliff. Twelve went down with her, including four women. We were the first ones to penetrate inside. We found one body."

I sat up. "You found a body–down since 1947?"

"The nose was pretty well gone, the eyes were gone, but a good part of his lips were still there. His skin, his hair, and his clothes were still there. The only thing that was missing, and we presume it was because of the boiler's explosion, were his arms from the elbows down. Had you known this person in life, you would have known him down there. He was that preserved."

"You didn't just leave it down, there did you?"

"When we got back ashore, we contacted a ranger at Isle Royale, and he went down with us. He had a wet suit on, but that compresses at depth to where it is paper thin so that there are no insulating qualities. The ranger took one look at the body–it was a gory thing–and he wanted nothing to do with it."

"We found out that if we brought the body up and we couldn't find anyone to take charge of the burial, we would be the ones responsible. Since the newspapers told about our finding the body, we had another problem. We were afraid the body would draw curiosity seekers: divers who weren't qualified to go that deep. We had to do something."

He paused. "We decided to go back down and drop the body off the stern. Off the cliff. That should have eliminated the problem."

"Did it?"

"Well, we went back down and took some pictures inside the wreck. Later, when we were looking at the slides, we noticed that on one of the bunks, with a lot of junk on it, was another body. You could see the legs, you could see the formation of the hind end, and the upper body and the arms reaching up. We couldn't see the head because it was covered."

"Are more bodies on board? Still down there?"

Bill looked at the fog lying thickly over the harbor. His thoughts seemed far away.

"There are boats that still haven't been discovered," he said. "For example, we know that the steel freighter, the *Benjamin Noble*, sank somewhere down the shore from us. The wreckage washed ashore. The crew was all lost when she went down in 1914 and she is believed to be sunk a short distance off Knife Island."

"I sailed right by there," I said.

"She was overloaded. The story was that at the ore docks here they had not enough steel for two boats and too much for one. When they got all that in her, she was so full that her anchor pockets were actually submerged."

"Why didn't the captain refuse?"

"Those were hard times and hard men. The captain was worried, but he figured if his boat had made it with someone else, he'd be branded as a coward. The *Noble* made it out of the harbor, into the lake and down to near the Duluth entryway. But a terrible storm came up and caught her. It was night. One of the lamps marking the entryway was washed out, so the captain couldn't tell where the channel was. He had to make a hard decision, and that was to turn around to head back to Two Harbors. He didn't make it and they haven't found him yet. The captain and all his crew vanished that night."

"Another mystery of Superior."

"There's a lot about Superior that we don't know yet, including a number of ships still down there, untouched since they went down."

"I'd think the wrecks would be as dangerous as the dive."

"They can be. Up at Isle Royale, the water is clear, and it's worthwhile going down. The wreck of the America lies up there. This diving club I was with neared the wreck just as another boatload of divers were getting out of their diving gear and starting toward shore. Somebody started shouting, 'Where's my brother, where's my brother?' They went back down, but they couldn't find him.

"They also didn't know the wreck very well, so they called in another diver who had a lot of experience on it. But by the time he got down, you knew the missing diver was gone. It was just a matter of finding the body. When they did, they found that the missing diver had gotten separated from his brother, had entered a room, got lost, and in panic, started flailing around and stirred up clouds of silt. He couldn't find his way back out."

Outside the guardhouse, the mist formed on the windows and the harbor lights grew halos.

"It's such an eerie feeling," Bill intoned, "when you start down from the surface and away from your boat and all you have is this line going below you. You pull your way down and then, there looms this huge manmade thing. One old stack has this hole that is so big you can just imagine something roaring up to grab you and drag you back. You look at the old portholes, you mind gets carried away, and you imagine an old, decomposed face staring back at you.

"The bodies are still down there. If they stay inside the wreck, protected from the fish, the bodies will still be well preserved. This body we found, we figured it was the engineer. The body was still firm and solid. I don't know if there is a petrifying process involved. We've got pictures of our divers holding the body up, one on either side. But the strange thing is that, when they opened the door in the compartment for the first time, it created a suction. We saw him moving in there, lifting and waving as if he were still alive.

"One gal was brave. She was studying to be an orthodontist. She went right up to him and she peeled off whatever was left of his lips and looked at his teeth. I wasn't that interested."

I had another sip of coffee. "Isn't a ship lying near where I'm berthed?"

"Right near the breakwater where you entered. It's the *Ely*, a three-masted schooner that got broken on the rocks in a storm in 1896. Fascinating wreck. Some original paint is still on the decks. That's how well preserved it is. I invited up a diver used to saltwater, and it amazed him. He told me that the wreck was fantastic, and he told me that any wreck he'd dived on in the ocean that there was practically nothing left because of the saltwater's erosion. 'But here,' he told me, 'I couldn't believe how good of a shape that vessel was in.'

"It's so impressive, the shipwrecks we have up here," Bill concluded. "It's quite a diver's paradise." ☀

7

Escape from the Island of Doom

--- ★★★ ---

Something wicked this way comes

7:30 A.M. FOG WISPED AROUND the tiny island harbor; the nearby hills of St. Ignace Island were wreathed in the gray stuff. The air was calm: on my transom, atop my boat's teak flagpole, my American flag drooped limply. Water lapped at my hull. I waited. Fog patches rolled in and out, like clouds of cotton candy.

An hour later I could make out the adjacent islands.

The fog was burning off.

Under power, I swung my 20-foot sailboat, *Persistence*, north around Agate Island, and headed southeast toward Talbot Island. I'd be on an inside channel–for a time. Then I'd be on Superior's open waters.

It was great to be free. I had been fog-bound for days in beautiful CPR Harbor, on St. Ignace Island. It was one of thousands of small islands dotting Lake Superior's Canadian north shore.

Environment Canada forecast a security alert: Small craft warning.

I was mindful of what a Canadian boater told me. "If you listen to them, they'll scare the hell out of you. And you'll never go anywhere."

I was restless. I wanted to get going. Someday, this rugged shoreline would be an enormous freshwater conservation area, one of the largest in the world. Now it was unrestricted and free. And so was I.

True, I'd have to pass by a famous–and ghostly–piece of rock with a bad reputation. Then I'd head out onto Superior's open waters before swinging up a rugged channel to the village of Rossport, Ontario. A piece of cake.

.... ❋ ....

As I sailed past Talbot Island, I took no chances and gave it a wide berth. It looked like just another rocky island out here in the midst of nowhere.

To the east were reefs that stretched underwater–dangerous enough that the Canadian government had to build Superior's first lighthouse here.

This was the legendary Island of Doom.

From my bouncing cockpit, I trained my binoculars on the desolate, wind-swept chunk of rock. I couldn't make out a piece of a lighthouse or even the rocky base where a structure might have stood. The islet is low; storms could have overrun it and swept away all signs of man.

Built in 1867, the first lighthouse was a white, wooden tower. It was illuminated by three kerosene lamps and maintained by a man named Perry. In his isolated post on the lonely island, the first lighthouse keeper on Superior was pretty much on his own–including finding his way back to civilization.

At the end of the first season around mid-December, Perry closed the station and began a voyage in a small sailboat to a trading post at the Nipigon River's mouth. He never made it.

They discovered his body the next spring on a beach beside his overturned boat. He was victim number one.

The next year, the lighthouse was built bigger so the keeper could stay on the island all winter. Capt. Thomas Lamphier, a veteran skipper of a Hudson's Bay schooner for 20 years, was hired as a keeper. He lived on the island with his wife.

After Superior froze over late in the fall, he died, leaving his grieving wife alone and isolated on the island. There was no way to get help. Since Talbot is all rock, she had no way of burying him. She did the only thing she could: she wrapped his body in canvas and placed him a short distance behind the lighthouse in a rock crevasse. All winter long, she lived on the isolated island with her husband's unburied corpse nearby.

It wasn't until the following spring that a group of Ojibway paddlers saw Mrs. Lamphier's urgent signals. They took the body by canoe to nearby Bowman Island, where they buried it. Atop his grave, they placed a small cross.

When the lighthouse service ship arrived on Talbot Island, the crew almost did not recognize Mrs. Lamphier. Her black hair had turned a ghastly white.

Tragedy also struck the third keeper, Andrew Hynes. At season's end in 1872, Hynes boarded up the lighthouse and set sail in a small boat for Fort William at Thunder Bay. At first, the weather was clear, but a storm erupted. Winds swept Superior, waves grew, and the temperature plummeted.

For 18 days, Hynes fought the seas in his open craft. He got as far as Silver Islet, about 60 miles to the west. At the small mining community, the half-frozen keeper lifted himself partway from his boat, told his name and a little of his horrifying voyage. Then he died.

There was no fourth keeper for the Island of Doom. The government abandoned the lighthouse in 1873–its macabre record unrivaled by any other Superior lighthouse.

The tower remained standing for years, but legends grew. Some said that when the fog rolled in, someone or something would beat against its wooden sides to warn those still out on the lake. Some saw a ghostly figure of a woman with long white hair wandering about the island. There was a curse on the island, and anyone who came too close would inherit its bad luck.

I did not see or hear anything as I sailed past the Island of Doom, but I still felt some kind of presence. This was a place with a bad history and a curse on it.

.... ❈ ....

Ahead in the mists lay 16 miles of open water. I slumped back in my inside steering seat. I had my remote control in hand, with my automatic helm doing all the steering. I checked my course on my GPS.

Let the boat do the work, I thought to myself. That's how I designed her.

Something dark rushed toward us in the water.

I threw the boat to one side and avoided it.

The next one hit the hull with a resounding thump. It traveled along the beam. It seemed an eternity before it cleared my spinning prop. Had it hit, I might have lost the motor.

I stood up. Ahead of the bow and stretching into the horizon were many little black things–bits of tree stumps, branches, and even logs.

This was the first time I'd come across any debris in Superior's clear water. Where had had all the logs and breakage had come?

I thought of the Island's curse. Bad luck had come to my boat; I had better be careful.

I slowed the engine and began to work our way through the log pack. I had my hand on the tiller, zigging and zagging the boat.

"Position ... what is your position?" the radio crackled. I did not know who was calling me, or even if it was for me, but I couldn't get to the radio.

My attention was on my deadly game of dodgem.

For many minutes, I paid careful attention to the deadly logs ahead of and around us.

Another log. Quick. Change. Slow the boat.

Bump. I hadn't expected that one. A scraping noise along the side of the hull.

I watched as the log bobbed off in our wake. I glanced ahead: more logs coming up. Two and threes. Big ones.

By the time I got past Moffitt strait, the water cleared up. We had passed through the debris field. And we had escaped the curse.

I checked below. Lifting the floorboards, I could not see water in my bilge. My cedar hull had held up, but I did not know how impact-resistant the three-eighths-inch cedar would be.

And I'd rather not find out.

.... ❀ ....

The wind started to blow from the southeast and the boat slowed and swayed with the gusts, creaking, groaning, and clanging. The waves were hitting us off our starboard bow, splashing some of their white caps aboard.

I glanced below just in time to see a slop of water shooting up through the open centerboard trunk.

A chill settled in my stomach. *Persistence* had entered Superior's open waters and already I was having problems.

Double-checking my chart, I was on a course of 102 degrees, heading easterly, doing 5.9 mph. I had just changed from a heading of 92 degrees off Grebe Point, trying to avoid a big pile of reefs off Beetle Point.

There was hope. An hour of this and I'd be heading into Simpson Strait, on my way to Lake Nipigon. I'd be in the protection of the islands.

I was putting down my chart when a white bank rolled in with the wind. All my landmarks disappeared.

Total fog. I could barely see beyond my bow.

My adrenalin surged again. A small voice inside my head warned:

Danger! You should get the heck out of here.

I shook my head, trying to center myself. Sailing Superior is as much a mind game as physical. Keep a psychological advantage–and do not give in to fear. Or panic.

I knew I had to concentrate.

Now... where was that bloody channel?

Not far ahead were the reefs off Simpson Island. It was one thing to look for them when you could see them and another to continue blindly toward them.

If I went too far, I'd run across more reefs off Battle Island.

I spread out my chart and worked my dividers. The bouncing ride was not helping. The sweat was dripping down from my face. Having my eye-glasses fog up was not helping either. I calculated positions and punched in additional landmarks; one to a point south of the channel, and more up the channel's mid-point. I hoped I got the numbers right.

In a shaky hand, I wrote the positions on the side of my chart. I nearly stabbed myself with the dividers.

OK, now I had it. The exact point where I should steer was landmark Morn 1, opposite Morn Point. Once this landmark came up, I would make my turn, avoiding the reefs off Morn and also off Battle Island. I'd head merrily northwesterly up the channel.

I peered ahead. But all I could see was the bow of my boat, plunging along, occasionally slinging up spray. The rest was fog and gray water.

I braced myself as the boat rolled about in the waves, one side, then the other. The Canadian paper chart which I had folded in quarters, swung back and forth from its holder like a pendulum.

The GPS was to the right of my nose; I could not miss it. The clock, with its oversize analog hands, was to my left, so I could keep track of time running for dead reckoning. Ahead of me were two compasses, which did not agree.

I knew that if I miscalculated, I'd be on the rocks before I could see them. I might not have time to turn.

It was past noon, but I had no appetite for food. My stomach was knotted up.

I didn't imagine there would be anyone else dumb enough to be running out here in the fog with me. Still, it didn't hurt to check.

"Security ... security," I broadcast on my VHF radio, identifying myself to the Canadian Coast Guard. "I am nearing the south entrance to the Simpson channel, encountering heavy fog and want to contact any boats in the vicinity."

Only static greeted me. I broadcast my security message several more times.

A voice came through the speaker: "We are sending out your warning and your heading." It was the Thunder Bay Coast Guard. They also told me there were a few fishing boats in several coves but staying put.

Good. I had the channel to myself, so I plugged on, flying low and slow.

My little GPS was giving me speed, heading, and coordinates. It told me how soon I'd get to the next landmark. There were several screens I had been using: one with an arrow on it telling me if I was on my heading or not.

But where was I? That bothered me. Too close to the edge of the island, and I'd be in some serious rocks. Too far west—more rocks.

Dummy! I could almost have kicked myself, for I realized that I had not used one screen on my GPS–the one that told me exactly what my position was, good within about 50 feet. I glanced upward in the fog at what must be the heavens and uttered a small thanks.

I clicked on the screen, and there I was. My position. Exactly.

It seemed to me I might be getting a little close to the rocks, so I edged northward off the lake a little more. With my dividers, I double-checked the landmark I had selected, and then triple checked it. A tense moment. When all the numbers aligned and the stars in the heavens agreed, I punched in my turn. The faithful Autohelm buzzed; the boat turned.

I crossed my fingers.

I watched the GPS numbers line up. I was, theoretically, west of Battle Island, entering the channel between Simpson Island and Salter Island.

The motion of the boat changed. I could feel the difference. The wind and the waves were now coming off my starboard aft quarter.

A white orb appeared above me in the gray sky. Below me, the waters turned blue.

The sun was burning the fog away. When I emerged from the fog, I was, miracle of miracles, right in the middle of the channel. Exactly where I should be. I could have kissed my little GPS unit. It had guided me unerringly off the lake.

By 2 p.m., as I neared the north end of Salter Island, a yellow sun beamed overhead; below me, the waters were calm and sparkling.

I was in Nipigon Bay. What a difference! Summer had returned; I began to perspire.

From my chart, I knew Barwis Reef lay dead ahead. I pulled out my binoculars to look for the reef marker, but I couldn't see anything. I stood in the cockpit, holding onto the swaying boom, searching the water.

According to my chart, there was supposed to be a flashing red light that marked the reefs. Nothing.

Out came the chart, the dividers, and the GPS, and I placed them on a towel in the cockpit. I calculated new landmarks to bypass the reef. It was now 3 p.m.; the wind out of the east had slowed my eastward passage to 4.9 mph.

Ahead lay the tree-topped islands of Rossport Harbor. My route was toward Quarry Island, a high, towering island. The sun was beating down on my back, and since I was wearing all my boating gear plus PFD and safety harness, I was perspiring. I also felt sleepy. Very sleepy.

I caught myself staring at a channel marker. Just staring. I yanked myself upright: I was guiding my boat toward a red, striped marker.

Reefs!

I yanked the tiller over, correcting my course. How stupid could you get? I almost had put us on the rocks.

We rounded the bend; ahead lay beautiful Rossport Harbor.

As I came closer to the municipal dock, I blinked twice in the sunlight. A large, white boat was tied alongside. I saw that a crew person was aboard.

"Where's the best place to tie up?" I yelled.

The woman made a motion of her head, as if to say, "this way," and walked over to one side. I tossed her my line–and we were inside the L-shaped dock, safe.

"Welcome to Rossport," she said. "Did you have a good trip?"

"A little fog."

"You get some of that around here," she said. ✸

8

The last of the steam tugboats

The Edna G.'s stormy adventures

THE VETERAN TUGBOAT CAPTAIN, Adolph Ojard, had a mariner's stiff bearing, silver hair and a steely-eyed gaze that looked like he belonged on the bridge. He loved the *Edna G.*, the old steam tugboat he sailed so many years.

"She's the last of the coal-burning tugboats, built in 1896," Capt. Ojard told me. " I've been with her 27 years; I'm retired now and so is she. She's on the registry of national historic places—one of the few floating ones."

"And can she burn coal!" He warmed to his subject. "Let me tell you about the time we had to go out after the *Joe Thompson*. She lost power about 18 miles from here, and I had to bring her in. We towed her back with her rudder cocked. By the time we got back to Two Harbors, my fireman had lost 19 pounds."

"She's fired by hand?"

"Sure. She's the only hand-fired coal burner around. We always kept a hundred ton in her, with her bunkers full."

I thought about the many boats this old tug had rescued along these rocky shores. "Is steam really good to power a boat?"

Capt. Ojard looked surprised. "When it comes to handling, it has diesel beat all to hell. It's faster. For example, when I want reverse, I've got it. But a diesel will take you 60 seconds."

"Doesn't it take time to get steam up?"

"In the old days, we had three crews and kept the fire up at all times. By hand firing, you can boost steam up in a hell of a hurry. We could get underway in a half hour."

"How fast will she go?"

"Well, she's 110-feet long with a beam of 23 feet and a draft of 15 feet 6 inches. The propeller is 9 feet in diameter with a 12-foot pitch. That works out to one revolution every 12 feet. At full 125 rpm., which is not too slow for steam, she'll cruise at 12 ½ knots and wear 14 ½ at full speed."

He paused: "Trouble is, at full speed, the fireman can't keep up. She burns roughly a ton of coal an hour."

Capt. Ojard glanced over the harbor to the big sea. "We didn't begrudge her anything. She got us there and back again. Let me tell you about one time in the winter we had to take her out. A fisherman went in the a.m. to tend his nets about 8 miles southeast of Two Harbors. It was in January. He was gone all day and his family got worried as night came on. He had ship-to-shore radio, but his family hadn't heard from him.

"They called me, and I got a crew together. Once we got outside the break wall, there was quite a sea on. We fought high waves and wind; my radar didn't work in the snowstorm. I tried to figure out where he'd be and try to reach him by radio. But every time I tried to receive his message, all I heard was a click. I figured things out and said, 'Frank, if you can hear me, click your button twice.'

"I heard two clicks. His battery was nearly gone, not enough to transmit his voice. But we got his clicks. Now the problem was one of finding him.

"I turned on my searchlight. 'Frank,' I said, 'when the searchlight is on you, click your button twice again.'

"We swung the light and when it was on him, I heard two clicks again. Now I knew what course he was on and headed toward him. He had been drifting all day and as we drew near, I saw that he had all sorts of garbage out as sea anchors – fish crates, five-gallon buckets—anything to hold the bow into the wind and keep him off the rocks. Remember we had a northeaster out there, with 15-foot seas, and the temperature was 5 degrees above zero.

"We worked our way up to him and the first thing he said was, 'Nice to see you.'

"But that was the end of the pleasantries. I tried to get him to transfer over to my boat, but I couldn't take him off. He had a covered steel fishing boat and wouldn't leave her, and so he crawled up on the bow and pulled the line we tossed him, and we towed him in. We had found him only a few miles from a storm-swept beach."

It had been that close. Navigation could be tricky. He and his beloved *Edna G.* had gone out to rescue even big ore boats. One, the *James Farrell*, had caught a northeaster and tried to get in but couldn't and was being carried to the rocks. Despite the storm, Capt. Ojard had maneuvered his tug alongside the giant ore boat and tossed up a line. But as he recalled, "By the time we got her stopped, her stern was so near the rocks the propeller was kicking up sticks."

That had been another close one.

"Do you sail on the lake these days?" I asked. "I mean, for yourself."

He shook his head. "I don't even own a boat. I spent all the time on one I want to. Now if I want to do some rocking, I'll get me a rocking chair." ❀

9

But the Nasmyth survived the storm

A giant ship meets its end as an old schooner barge lives on

TWO 1,720-FOOT-LONG CONCRETE PIERS jut from Duluth's inner harbor into Lake Superior. Between them lies a shipping channel with a width of 300 feet, from pier to pier. There is a walkway on the north pier. To stroll along its length is to change from land to inland ocean, from the quiet waters of the harbor to the roil of a freshwater sea. Out at the end, where the lighthouses mark the way for the salties and the ore boats, the air is clean. Breezes bring you the scent of fresh water

I can't imagine that one of the lake's worst shipwrecks happened here. The wreck site was near the north pier where I am standing – maybe 100 feet away – and only about 700 feet from the rocky shore.

One cold, blustery November day, this tragedy happened in full view of the city. Thousands of onlookers watched in horror, bonfires burned on the beach, lifesavers and their equipment stood by as men aboard the stricken vessel cried for rescue to the people on shore. But no one could help.

One of the worst storms to hit Superior had caught the *Mataafa.* The famed northeaster of 1905 had gale force winds and mountainous seas. It was the worst day in the history of the Port of Duluth.

About 3:30 p.m. on a clear but cold November 27 that the *Mataafa*, a

430-foot long steel boat, steamed through these long entryway piers and onto Superior's calm waters. Only six years old and easily handling her cargo of iron ore, the *Mataafa* was towing her consort schooner barge, the 366-foot steel *James Nasmyth*. Both were their way across Lake Superior in one of their last runs of the season.

The forecast for Thanksgiving Day was ominous, but every lake captain knew the lake was changeable. If they took a chance, maybe they could get well away from the Head of the Lakes before a predicted storm arrived. The common wisdom was, if you listened to everything the weather bureau told you, you'd go nowhere.

They were on the northern trek, a favored route of the lake captains when storms were imminent. This meant hugging the Minnesota North shore and following the lake around its natural curvature to the east, within sailing distance of the few ports that were available. It was a rugged, inhospitable shore but they could duck in out of the weather at several places, if they had to. They could find safety behind Isle Royale. As they got into the northernmost arc of the lake, they could get some shelter from the shoreline itself if they were careful.

Luck was always a factor in Lake Superior shipping but about four hours later, when the *Mataafa* and the schooner barge *Nasmyth* were near Two Harbors, Minnesota, a savage winter storm exploded. It was a dreaded winter northeaster.

The winds howled the length of the lake at gale force, the seas built, and snow and sleet slanted across the dangerous waters. Visibility dropped.

Between bursts of snow and spume, the *Mataafa's* captain, R. F. Humble, could not see the aft section of his own ship, much less the following barge, the *Nasmyth*. Deckhands complained they couldn't see their own hands at the end of their arms because of the snow and sleet.

Worse, the big ship's 1,400 horsepower engine could not make any headway into the storm. At engine full ahead, the *Mataafa* labored in the waves, bashing through the troughs, but after 10 hours of fighting the storm, she was taking a terrific beating, with her wheel—her propeller— sometimes coming part way out of the water.

She was in a fight for her life.

The entryway to the harbor at Two Harbors was always a tricky one to traverse even in clear weather for a ship this size. In extreme conditions with a heavy seaway and gale-force winds and towing a huge barge, Capt. Humble could not even attempt to enter the small port of refuge.

His only salvation lay in the harbor he left many hours before: Duluth. But that meant getting through the Duluth entryway, known as "running the chute." It was very tricky in harsh conditions.

Before he could do that, he had to turn his vessel with his tow.

That was a harrowing business. Turning a large steel carrier in heavy seas could mean getting broadsided by waves, pushed down on her beam ends, and risking capsizing. But the *Mataafa* was also towing a heavy barge.

At about 8:30 a.m., Capt. Humble waited until one wave train passed, then called for full starboard rudder. The two boats turned and ran with the waves and wind.

At noon, Capt. Humble saw the skyline of Duluth. The snow and sleet had let up and he now had visibility enough to make out the Duluth canal ahead of the plunging boats.

He had to face another decision: What to do with his tow? There were men aboard the unpowered schooner barge.

It was unlikely that both the *Mataafa* and the *Nasmyth* could both make it through the narrow ship canal.

Onboard the schooner barge, the men saw the *Mataafa* slow and its crew work the tow lines. They could not hear what the crew was hollering over the noise of the wind and the waves.

They were being abandoned.

The *Mataafa* crew released their straining towline and left the *Nasmyth* to its own survival in treacherous seas. They were alone.

The *Nasmyth's* crew dropped anchors. With heavy water scouring the deck, the schooner barge's bow swung into the wind and the waves. Their ship was working hard.

They hung from their anchors about two miles from the Duluth entryway, where they saw the *Mataafa* steaming hard for safety.

The bargemen had done all they could. Now they had to slug it out alone with the storm on the open waters. Waves slashed across the bow and ice began to form on the slippery decks.

The *Nasmyth* pounded in the monstrous waves and their crew felt every blow. A feeling of abandonment came over them.

.... ✳ ....

Waves overran the stone piers; spume shot up in the air. There was a heavy crosswind— estimated to be up at around 70 mph— whirling up bits of snow.

Running "the chute" was always hazardous but now it looked almost impossible. There were not only cross currents swirling about the pier heads, but in this weather, with storm surge piling up in the inner harbor, there was also the problem of the back surge, where currents ran back through the channel toward the lake, making piloting tricky.

The *Mataafa* could get caught by the wind, waves and currents – and maybe all three. But to stay on the lake meant certain death.

.... ✳ ....

Black smoke billowing, the *Mataafa* drove forward with engines full ahead to gain the protection of the stone piers. Speed was important.

But partway in, the driving ship was overtaken by a huge wave, lifting its aft section. Even steel ships of 4,800 tons move up and down in the waves, and as the storm wave raised the aft section, the bow plunged downward into the entryway's bottom. The *Mataafa* dug into the sand and mud. Its course deflected, it slammed its starboard bow into the north pier. Steel bow plates screamed against the concrete.

The *Mataafa* tried to maneuver, but the storm jammed the rudder. Then the engines stopped. They had no power. No ability to maneuver.

Another set of waves caught the aft section, levering the giant boat like a toy. Her stern slewed off, her starboard midsection struck the pier of the harbor breakwater.

The full fury of the lake pounced upon her and she was pushed back into the lake. Her bow spun around. Spray flew higher than her bridge as the *Mataafa* pivoted about the pierhead, her bow heading into the wind and waves. Waves smashed the full length of the stricken vessel, overrunning the spar deck.

The *Mataafa* did a half a circle. She ended up on the rocks about 600 feet from shore and about 100 feet from the North Pier.

Capt. Humble heard a series of low rumbles and a cracking noise. The big ship developed a hump in its mid deck section: her back had been broken in two places. Water sliced through the cracked hull. Ice was getting a deadly grip.

As night descended, people in waterfront hotels peered out at the stricken ship. Thousands more braved the storm to fight their way to the water's edge, where they lighted bonfires and maintained a vigil. They saw the two groups of men aboard, only about 600 feet away. Some were in the forward section; more crew were in the aft section.

The men were isolated by the open spar deck that was regularly swept by powerful waves.

.... ❈ ....

From shore, Life Savers tried to launch a lifeboat, but in the roaring waves, rescue was impossible; no lifeboat could survive the wild waters. They tried again and again. But they had to wait.

As the long night deepened, the temperature dropped to 13 degrees below zero.

Onboard, three men fought their way from the aft cabin along the icy deck to the forward cabin. A fourth man attempted to cross the storm-lashed open deck three times, but each time he was almost washed overboard. On his fourth try, he turned to see black water roar toward him. He bellowed a cry of "no!" and then retreated to the aft cabin.

At dawn, when the temperature was 20 degrees below, the wind had stilled a little and the seas had calmed. Rescuers in a lifeboat rowed out to the *Mataafa*.

They found the men in the forward section huddled together, frost-bitten but alive. They had torn paneling off the cabin and lit a small fire to keep warm, with the captain admonishing them to keep moving. "We danced all night to the sound of that terrible gurgling water," one man said. They were chilled, frostbitten—but alive.

Those who sought shelter in the aft cabin were so entombed in ice that their bodies had to be chopped out with axes. One man had stuffed himself in a ventilator so he could watch the shore, only a short distance away, as he slowly froze to death, his eyes wide open.

In full view of a city, a steel ship and its crew could not be rescued from Superior's fury. In that terrible storm of 1905, 29 other ships had gone down.

Out on the lake, after the waves had subsided, the men on board the old schooner barge cautiously opened the hatches. They found their humble sailing craft still seaworthy and bobbing way in the chop. Rescue came a little later as another boat ventured out and towed them into the safety of the harbor.

No one lost his life on the old boat. The *Nasmyth* had survived.

10

The last battle of the Grampa Woo

One of the most harrowing at-sea rescues in Great Lakes history

IN THE PRE-DAWN DARKNESS of October 30, 1996, Capt. Dana Kollars awakened with an uneasy premonition. It was late in the season and nearing the time of Lake Superior's dreaded gales of November. The *Grampa Woo* should have headed south long ago, but she was still moored in Grand Portage Bay.

Outside his home in Beaver Bay, the wind was starting to moan. Still half asleep and fighting off traces of exhaustion, he drove north on Hwy. 61. In the headlight's glare, fall leaves skittered across the road; gusts of wind rocked his car.

Out on the lake, black hills were forming, topped with streaks of white.

A weather system had moved in early. The barometer was falling to its lowest point in the area's history.

He pushed his speeding car harder.

By daybreak, Capt. Dana stood shivering on the end of the dock at Voyageur's Marina. Waves chopped at the pier; wind drove spray horizontally.

Less than a mile away, his beautiful, 110-foot long aluminum vessel *Grampa Woo* rode the gusts with aplomb, her sleek bow cocked to windward. The *Woo* was holding steady at her 4,000-pound mooring off Grand Portage Island.

A vessel designed for offshore ocean use, the *Grampa Woo* hauled workers and equipment out to Gulf of Mexico oil rigs. Later, she made regular trips on the East Coast as a charter fishing boat and as a whale watcher. When Capt. Dana located her, he converted her to take passengers out on pleasure cruises on the North Shore of Lake Superior. She was his million-dollar retirement plan, and he and his wife, ChunAe, were so proud of her they named her for ChunAe's much loved Korean father.

Now that the *Grampa Woo* had ended her first season on Superior's North Shore, Capt. Dana was doing maintenance work, servicing her engines and outfitting her for her trip south. She was at Dana's mooring in Grand Portage Bay off Grand Portage Island, rather than at her regular dock at Beaver Bay, about 150 miles to the south. Capt. Dana had planned to sail east toward Sault Ste. Marie, and then, exiting the Great Lakes, get on the rivers leading south to the Gulf of Mexico.

Six months earlier, Capt. Dana had ordered a new set of wheels to replace the *Woo's* three mismatched propellers. On the port was a 30-inch diameter 32-pitch four-bladed propeller. Her center prop was 30-inch diameter, 31-pitch three-bladed. But the starboard was 32-inch diameter, 32-pitch four bladed. Because the wheels were mismatched, the port engine worked under a heavy load and ran at a higher temperature than the others. With a 2,400-mile trip to the Gulf, Capt. Dana wanted matched props that would let his engines pull an equal load, giving his beloved *Woo* better speed and economy with less vibration.

The prop's expected delivery date had been September 1, but Capt. Dana received an explanation that the foundry in Mexico was just casting them. Weeks later, when he checked again, he was told the props had been held up in customs. Still later, he was told the props had been misplaced in shipment. After waiting 60 days past the expected delivery date, the shipping company called to say the props were enroute, and, at his request, had faxed a notification of the delivery date. When he got written confirmation, Capt. Dana sent divers underwater in the chilly bay to take the propellers off the *Woo*.

Today, the *Woo* was without propulsion. Her bare shafts waited for the new propellers.

The ship's inflatable Zodiac was at the dock, so Capt. Dana told deck hand Robin Sivill to gas up its 35-h.p. outboard engine. Satisfied everything was still under control, he strolled off the dock to talk with Kek Melby, owner and operator of Voyageur's Marina.

The *Grampa Woo* was moored in the shelter of Grand Portage Island. Inside the harbor and behind the island, the *Woo* would get protection from the northeast winds that cpuld sweep the length of Lake Superior and pile up huge waves. His boat was tethered to the bottom by a hundred feet of heavy chain and 120 feet of one-and a half-inch thick line. Capt. Dana's mooring was a massive 4,000 chunk of steel, on which re-rod spikes were welded. Some locals had jokingly told him his mooring was "over engineered."

"Captain," the deck hand yelled, "*Grampa Woo* is moving."

"Just shifting on her mooring," Capt. Dana responded. "Don't worry about it."

"She's moving!"

.... ❋ ....

They dashed to the dock. Capt. Dana saw that the wind had increased and was blowing straight out of the west. The gusts were so strong that they shoved half-filled 55-gallon oil drums off the pier.

As Capt. Dana watched in amazement, the *Woo* slipped 50 feet.

Throwing the lines off the inflatable, they headed out into the shallow bay to get to the *Woo*. The knife-like wind was on their starboard beam; the bay was alive with waves. The speeding Zodiac took stinging spray aboard, dousing Capt. Dana and Robin, who were dressed in light jackets.

Halfway to the *Woo*, the outboard started to sputter and to miss.

In their haste to get to the *Woo*, they did not don special clothing or carry a radio to get help. They had jumped aboard the small inflatable in their shore-side clothing, protected only by light jackets. They were exposed to the sweep of the wind and doused by waves in the bay. If the engine stalled or quit, they'd be swept out the harbor's entryway into the raging lake.

Faltering, but outboard still running, the inflatable bumped alongside the *Woo*. The two climbed on board.

"That felt really good," Capt. Dana recalled. "It felt good to be on a nice, big ship."

Onboard, they fired up the engines. Although the *Woo* had no propellers, the power gave them the ship's electronics, including depth sounder, knot meter, global positioning system (GPS) and the all-important VHF—their radio lifeline.

They threw the ship's 80-pound Danforth overboard and another, smaller anchor; they increased the scope on the mooring. On the bow, they could see the anchors and the mooring line grow taut—and hold.

But the *Woo* had slipped 300 yards into 38 feet of water. With 200 feet of line out, they did not have enough scope on the anchors or the mooring to hold.

"And I knew that," Capt. Dana recalled later. "My other hope was that the second anchor would hold, and we would be able to increase the scope on that."

A wall of wind hit the vessel and they could feel the *Grampa Woo* break loose. Dragging its heavy mooring and two large anchors across the bottom, the *Woo* headed through the harbor and out into the deep waters of Superior. The seas built.

In a matter of minutes, the bottom under the *Woo* became 80, then 120 feet. Finally, the depth sounder did not register the depth—it was too great. They were on Superior's open waters.

They threw out a sea anchor and the parachute-like device held the bow into the wind. In the pilothouse, Capt. Dana checked the GPS and did some quick calculations. Despite her anchors, the sea anchor and the mooring, the *Woo* was moving backward at 4 1/2 knots (about 5 miles an hour) under wind power alone. She was heading for the reefs of Isle Royale.

They'd hit in several hours.

On the VHF radio, Capt. Dana put in a distress call to Voyageur's Marina, alerting his friend Kek that they had blown out to sea. Kek told them he'd launch his 28-foot boat. It was a brave offer.

"You should stay," Capt. Dana advised him. "The seas are too high, and the wind is too strong. You'll accomplish nothing except endangering your own life."

There was no other boat at Grand Portage that could help. The *Woo* was not in Canadian waters and the nearest U.S. Coast Guard station with a boat big enough was in Duluth, Minnesota—over 150 miles away, an eternity in these seas.

.... ✿ ....

Something appeared in the distance, about eight to ten miles away. Capt. Dana made out an ore boat plowing through the heavy seas. She was the 1,000-foot-long *Walter J. McCarthy*, out of Duluth.

Capt. Dana, a retired U.S. Army officer who had once trained for the priesthood, said later: "You know, there are times when you think everything is gone, and then God blesses you."

Capt. Dana hailed the ore boat on the VHF. With relief, he saw the giant alter course toward the drifting Woo.

In the heavy seas, maneuvering the big ore boat was difficult. On the second pass, the *McCarthy* was able to put her mass between the high seas and the *Woo*.

The captain of the *McCarthy* requested that Capt. Dana and Robin leave the *Grampa Woo* and board the ore boat. Dana recalled later, "In my heart I thought I owed my vessel the opportunity to get a tow."

Both sailors elected to stay with their boat.

"We felt a little bit like the duckling up against the hen and it was a comforting feeling," Dana recalled later.

The *McCarthy* sent down a three-inch thick cable. By the time they had secured the towline to the *Woo*, the smaller boat had slipped to the stern of the McCarthy and the *Woo* pitched and pounded, on ten-foot bobs.

As Capt. Dana later recalled: "I'm a happy man. I've got a nice tow line, tucked in behind the stern of a great, beautiful thousand-foot ore boat, and headed for Thunder Bay, Canada."

Once the *Woo* got the towline, Capt. Dana and Robin tried to retrieve the anchors still dragging in the water. They discovered the lines were frozen; their only option was to cut them off.

Half frozen themselves, they scrambled back to the *Woo's* pilot house. The rolling and bumping between the ships had battered the Woo's side and tore up her bowsprit, but the captain and crew were secure in their ship.

"Of course, we had heavy seas, but as long as I could see that the tow line was taut, I was happy," Capt. Dana recalled.

.... ✿ ....

As darkness fell, the storm grew worse. A snowstorm swirled about, hampering visibility. They passed the international border and were making passage in Canadian waters, nearing the line of islands that guarded the stormy entrance to Thunder Bay.

On his cell phone, Capt. Dana called Thunder Bay Marine Services, Ltd., to have a tugboat meet the *Woo* by Pie Island, "and tow us into the marina, and tuck us into bed in a nice dock."

He also called the Thunder Bay Coast Guard, which said it would come out and render assistance, if it possibly could.

For the first time in hours, Capt. Dana felt a flush of success. He was under tow, he had a tug coming out to finish the voyage, and the Coast Guard was standing by.

He took time to call and reassure his wife, ChunAe, who was worried, and to talk to his son in Duluth, who by now had heard about the accident on television.

The *Woo's* motion changed. She lost speed.

Putting down his cell phone, Capt. Dana peered out the iced-over pilot house window and saw new trouble. After being stretched in hammering seas and frayed against the broken bowsprit, the three-inch towline had snapped.

Capt. Dana could only stare into the growing darkness to see the thousand footer's brightly lit ten-story structure grow smaller and smaller in the distance.

In 20-foot seas, they were alone once more. Trouble was building.

The helpless *Woo* was drifting without power. With the loss of her sea anchor, the *Grampa Woo* was no longer bow-to the seas but cocking broadside to the waves, a dangerous position. She was rolling in the troughs, presenting her vulnerable sides to the onrushing waves.

Time and options were running out. The *Grampa Woo* could drift in the heavy seas, until a rogue wave caught her beam to and pulled her over or she could drift until she slammed up against the sharp reefs and rocky shoreline of Isle Royale. And sank.

❋

It was dark. Snow was coming down hard and heavy. Ice was forming on deck.

.... ※ ....

The Canadian Coast Guard's 44-foot *Wesfort* fought her way to the south, taking westerly winds on her starboard beam. It was a rough night on Thunder Bay. The veteran patrol-and-rescue vessel was encountering unexpected problems.

Chief Coxswain Bob King and crewmembers Inga Thorsteinson and Willie Trognitz saw ice building up on their ship's mast and topsides.

The *Wesfort* was becoming top heavy. If she iced up enough, she might not be able to right herself. She was not designed for these seas nor this kind of weather.

Capt. Gerry Dawson, aboard the *Glenada,* also was having problems. The 76-foot Canadian tug was more suited for the harbor than the open waters. As she pushed her way across Thunder Bay's reef-strewn waters, her low stern was awash with waves; her bow scooped up heavy water.

Below decks, Jack Olson, a four-decade veteran of Superior, was manning the engine room despite diesel fumes and the vessel's pitching and rolling. For the first time in his life, he was becoming seasick.

At 7 p.m., the *Glenada* reached the northeast tip of Pie Island and waited in the storm-tossed darkness. After about a half an hour, through swirls of snow, Capt. Gerry could make out the lights of the big ore boat, making its turn into Thunder Bay.

Off the *McCarthy's* stern, the lights of the *Woo* came into view. Then the Canadian tug captain stared in disbelief. The two dim lights were growing apart.

The distance between the *McCarthy* and the *Woo* was increasing. It became obvious to him that the towline had snapped. The *Woo* was adrift, beam-to in the twenty-two-foot seas off the notorious Thunder Cape.

The *Glenada* charged out to the rescue.

.... ※ ....

The *Wesfort* continued to fight its way to the *Woo*, with crew member Inga Thorsteinson at the helm. The Coast Guard vessel's decks, superstructure and mast were now so heavily coated with ice that she was rolling down to nearly 90 degrees, practically on her side.

She had a bad hesitation before she came back up—top-heavy and in trouble. Everyone aboard knew the Canadian vessel was exceeding her roll capacity. They pressed on.

Onboard the tug *Glenada*, deck hand Jim Harding donned a survival suit and struggled out into the spray. Beneath his running shoes, he found that the deck was so thick with wet ice that he couldn't stand upright. He looked around: Everything was ice coated: railings, rigging and the wheelhouse. Even the windows were iced up.

Jim dropped to his hands and knees and crawled forward to the towing lines. But he couldn't uncoil a single one. All were frozen to the deck.

.... ❁ ....

Capt. Dana saw the *Glenada*, ice covered and fighting the beam seas, come into range—and pass him by. She circled several times, but never came close enough for a rescue attempt.

The tug was having its own problems. The crew couldn't find a towing line it could use. All were frozen to the deck.

But the *Woo* had a large spool of line sheltered inside the main salon. It was a three-fourths-inch diameter polypropylene line, the kind that floats.

Capt. Dana and Robin dragged it onto the ice-covered bow, and after the tug made three more passes, they tossed it in the churning water. It floated downwind. On the *Glenada*, deck hand Jim caught the line, wrestled it up to the tug's bit and secured it.

But the stormy seas soon parted the heavy line.

The *Woo* was adrift again.

.... ❁ ....

With the *Glenada's* wheelhouse iced over, Capt. Gerry's only vision was through a three-inch wide area blasted clear with a defroster. Anxiously, he scanned the iced-over bow, but couldn't see his deck hand.

He grew worried. If Jim slipped into the high seas, he would have little chance of survival.

Unknown to the captain, Jim was just outside the wheelhouse, hanging on to the icy tow bollards. His legs went afloat when the seas cascaded on deck.

As the *Glenada* began to turn, Jim felt the position of wind and the waves change. He pulled himself along a handrail to the wheelhouse, and reaching up with his wedding ring, tapped the glass.

Hearing the tapping, Capt. Gerry saw a hand waving outside the defrosted hole. He yanked open the pilot house door.

Jim Harding, half frozen and rimmed with spray ice, tumbled in.

.... ❋ ....

Winds clocked out of the west at 90 miles an hour and the seas were the worst they had been.

The tug carved through the waves, her topsides iced up. At 7 p.m., Capt. Gerry spun the wheel. The *Glenada* turned for one desperate—and final—attempt.

In the 22-foot seas, Capt. Gerry took a bearing through his peep hole, aimed his tugboat's massive bow at the *Woo*, and gave her power.

He would have to maneuver the *Glenada* so that both she and the *Woo* were in the troughs of the waves, with both boats rising and falling at the same frequency.

When he was close enough, the captain gunned the engine to pinion her against the *Woo*. With a bang, The *Glenada's* bow shoved against the *Woo's* stern hard enough to push in the aft deck railings. The two boats were jammed together by the tug's power.

On the *Woo's* deck, Capt. Dana and Robin balanced themselves on the bouncing rail. Above them, the *Glenada's* bow lunged up and down. It would be a tricky maneuver.

Capt. Dana jumped. On the *Glenada's* bow, deck hand Jim Harding reached down and pulled Capt. Dana, and then Robin, onboard.

"The deck was completely iced," Capt. Dana recalled. "We slid on board and as we slipped down near the wheelhouse door, we grabbed the door, and crawled in."

The *Grampa Woo* was now alone and adrift.

.... ❋ ....

The *Glenada* and the *Wesfort* fought their way eastward, past the Thunder Cape, and swung into the protection of a low, flat island. Without bothering to anchor, Capt. Gerry ran the *Glenada's* bow onto Tee Harbor's gravel beach. A short while later, the Canadian Coast Guard vessel came alongside.

In a secure harbor, with both engines running, they waited out the storm. Onboard the rescue tug, the *Woo's* Capt. Dana and Robin borrowed dry clothes from the crew.

As they stripped out of their wet clothing, Capt. Dana made a curious discovery. He saw Robin pull a damp, brown-colored object from the inside of his jacket.

"What's that?" Capt. Dana asked.

Robin grinned, "Oatmeal."

Capt. Dana had to chuckle. Just before they abandoned ship, Robin had managed to disappear for a moment. It was to make a quick stop below to scoop up the teddy bear. Oatmeal, a special memento of a former girlfriend, became the third survivor of the *Woo*.

.... ❁ ....

It took days before the big lake calmed enough for them to sail back to Thunder Bay. When they arrived, the old port city gave them a hearty welcome and lavished praise on the heroic work of the crew of the tug and the Coast Guard vessel.

The *Glenada's* crew was awarded the Governor General's Medal of Bravery, one of the highest accolades Canada can bestow. The Thunder Bay Coast Guard crew received commendations for seamanship and bravery in what was described as "one of the most harrowing at-sea rescues in recent Great Lakes History."

.... ❁ ....

Days later, the Coast Guard took Capt. Dana out to see his beloved ship. She had gone ashore on the rocks to the north and west of Passage Island, off Isle Royale.

"Just 400 yards, just 400 yards to the south, and *Grampa Woo* would have missed Passage Island," Capt. Dana said. "She would have been afloat the next day or two. We could have gone out and taken her back ashore."

From the sea, she looked salvageable, as though she just needed a tow off the rocks. But a closer inspection showed that she was crumpled up on her side and impaled on the rocks, her port side ripped open.

A few days later, a storm finished the job.

The once-proud ship was in pieces, battered and stripped bare as she lay on the bottom. Half-inch aluminum was ripped as if it were paper. Heavy diesels had been torn from the vessel, and everything on them was gone pumps, valve covers, and belts.

The largest single piece, the wheelhouse, was carried 150 feet away from the rest of the wreck. It was nearly intact, sitting upright on bottom – as if it were waiting for its captain to come aboard and sail away.

················· ❀ ·················

Several days after wreck of the *Grampa Woo*, ChunAe received a telephone call from the shipping company. They told her they had a large package addressed to her.

It was COD for $4,200 – the three propellers, ready at last.

The shipper wanted to know when to deliver them.

She was able to handle that call with some briskness.

················· ❀ ·················

Years later, it took a trip of 2,000 miles to bring the new boat from the Gulf of Mexico. They voyaged up the rivers and waterways linking the middle of the continent, and across Superior—back to their beloved North Shore.

The route up from the Gulf of Mexico follows three Great Lakes, half a dozen states, and several rivers and waterways. Coming up from the Gulf of Mexico, *Grampa Woo II* entered the Tombigbee Waterway in Mobile, Alabama, went north on the Tennessee River to the Ohio River, in Kentucky, cruised southwestward a short distance on the Ohio River, entered the Mississippi River at Cairo, Illinois, and cruised northward. Up from St. Louis, Missouri, she entered the Illinois River and sailed to Chicago.

Here she entered Lake Michigan, cruised northward the length of the Great Lake, crossed over to Lake Huron, swung westward to the locks at Sault Ste. Marie, and then sailed westward on Lake Superior to the North Shore.

In a special place of honor, was the ship's mascot, "Oatmeal."

ChunAe, Capt. Dana, and Robin Sivill were happy. Like the *Woo* before her, the *Grampa Woo II* was a heavy-weather boat designed to service offshore oil rigs. She was longer at 115 feet, but also aluminum hulled and powered by three big diesel engines. With an enclosed dining area, private suites, and lots of seating, the beautiful ship also would go into service along the North Shore.

In the morning light, Capt. Dana slowed the powerful engines as he neared the four-mile gap between Isle Royale and Passage Island. The white ship followed the rocky coastline 400 feet and paused offshore, engines beating.

Beyond them, in pieces on the rocks and underwater, lay the remains of the original *Grampa Woo*.

It was ChunAe's first visit to the wreck site. With tears in her eyes, she bowed her head and dropped a single, white flower into the water.

Then they sailed away.

························ ❀ ························

The last chapter in the saga of the *Grampa Woo* came when the U.S. National Park Service demanded the removal of the wreck from the park island. Though Isle Royale has ten major wrecks underwater, the wreck of the *Woo* fell under "dumping of trash, debris, and those sorts of things," according to the park's chief ranger, who was quoted as saying that federal laws demanded the boat's removal.

All traces of the wreck had to be obliterated to a depth of 130 feet.

It was fitting that the last remains of the *Grampa Woo* were removed by the captain who did so much to save its crew. Capt. Gerry Dawson sailed his tug with three barges over to Passage Island, and with the help of divers, pulled the last pieces of the *Woo* from the water.

Her 45 tons of wreckage were sold for scrap metal.

························ ❀ ························

It was late in the afternoon on Superior as I took a long, hard look at nearby Grand Portage Island. I was aboard my own 20-foot centerboard sloop, *Persistence*, and I was weather-bound in my northward sail toward the mouth of Thunder Bay. Though the island was wreathed in heavy fog, I tried to imagine a beautiful white boat moored just off the island. It wasn't there anymore—nor would it ever return.

The *Grampa Woo* had followed an almost unbelievable sequence of improbable mishaps and just plain bad luck. Had Capt. Dana not removed the propellers when he did, the ship could have maneuvered under power against the blast of the wind. If the wheels arrived when they were scheduled, the *Woo* would have been on her way south. Had the wind not blown from the west, the *Woo* would not have been carried out of the harbor. That mooring also was protected from northwest and southwest winds. But the fickle winds blew out of the west—howling along the rugged North Shore, across the spit of land guarding the harbor, and exiting the gap between Grand Portage Island and Hat Point. As the captain later told me, if the wind had blown from nearly any other direction, the *Woo* would have gone into shallow water and survived, or, another way, ended up on a reef, but afloat. Only a 20-degree difference of direction would have saved her.

There had been more bad luck: Had the mooring held, or her anchors dug in, she would still be safe. Had the tow line off the *McCarthy* not chafed through, the ore boat would have towed the *Woo* safely inside the protection of Thunder Bay's breakwaters. Had the tow lines from the tug, *Glenada*, not been frozen to the deck, the *Woo* would have had a wild trip up Thunder Bay, but she would have survived. Had her final, unpiloted course been just one degree different, she would have blown clear of Passage Island, sailed through the strait, and merely drifted at sea until Capt. Dana could tow her back to safety.

It was an overwhelming tragedy, a series of events that ultimately went wrong—one by one.

Everything that could have been done was. Everything that was done failed.

The *Woo* had protected its crew. They survived. But in the end, the Big Lake had claimed yet another victim: The big boat itself. ❀

11

The mystery ship from 19 fathoms

---☆☆☆---

Divers bring up an ancient schooner

IT HAD BEEN A WARM JUNE DAY in 1864 when the *Alvin Clark* coasted past Death's Door Passage, to the north of Wisconsin's famous Door Peninsula. Entering the wide sweep of Green Bay, the topsail schooner was running behind a southwesterly wind, heading under full sail for Oconto, Wisconsin.

She was a centerboard vessel, whose swing keel could be raised or lowered. That made it possible for her to wiggle into undeveloped ports and shallow harbors to pick up and deliver cargoes. With her raked wooden masts, the bluff-bowed schooner had been sailing the Great Lakes for 18 years. Today's run was to pick up a load of lumber.

Two days out of Chicago, and sailing without cargo, Capt. Durnin looked over Green Bay's sparkling waters. He'd made satisfactory progress so far, but the wind had headed the small schooner. As he rounded Chambers Island, he figured he'd have to tack his way into the lumber port north of the city of Green Bay.

The short, stocky skipper shook his head. It was not like the bustling port of Chicago, with big city newspapers that always got the latest news. Capt. Durnin had been following progress of the Civil War; the exciting news was that President Abraham Lincoln had appointed a new general, Ulysses S. Grant, to be Commander of all Union Forces. Maybe that'd turn the tide of battle. The North was losing.

During the Civil War, good crew members were hard to find: The *Clark* had to sail out of Chicago shorthanded. Usually, she carried a captain, mate, cook, and four seamen, which is enough for a vessel of this size and complexity. But now she was manned only by the captain, a first mate, a two-man crew, besides one passenger who was working his passage. She could not even rustle up a cook this sailing season.

One of the crew was a young Canadian, Michael Cray, from Toronto, an able-bodied seaman who had already served one year in the Union Army. He still wore his threadbare blue army tunic onboard, but he had already served out his term of enlistment. Cray was safe from the draft.

All were proud to be aboard the *Clark*, a 220-ton vessel, one of only 270 sailing vessels on all the Great Lakes. Launched in 1846, and built of white oak, she had an overall length of 113 feet, including her long jib boom. Her masts were raked; her main mast soared 95 feet above her deck. Although a topsail schooner, she could be mistaken for a brigantine since she had her three-piece foremast square rigged, from course to topgallant. In a following wind, she could spread square sails and scoot along. She could carry 8,000 square feet of sail.

As they neared the northeast point of Chambers Island, Capt. Durnin looked up to check the set of the sails. They were as close hauled as he could get them. He'd keep the square sails up as long as they drew. If the wind changed, he'd send the crew aloft to take in the square sails and start tacking. He checked the set of the mainsheet. It was drawing well on its 58-foot boom.

By late afternoon, a cloud formation had built in the northeast. Capt. Durnin studied the dark horizon with care: this was infamous Green Bay. Thunderstorms with gale-force winds could spring up with suddenness and violence. The lake could develop a towering, vicious chop with short distances between wave crests. Like most lake captains, Capt. Durnin had a lot of respect for storms on Green Bay.

But the heavy weather appeared to be a passing rainstorm—no reason to shorten sail, the *Clark* was making good time to the southwest and with luck she'd make the mouth of the Oconto River by nightfall.

Within minutes, heavy clouds multiplied, blacking out the horizon to the northeast. On the shore, a squall tore up trees by the roots and downed fences. Rain and hail reached the *Clark*, followed by gale force winds.

Capt. Durnin put the helm down and shouted a warning to the crew to loosen the sheets. But as the *Clark* turned, her sails caught the wind and filled bar taut. The centerboard schooner rolled over on her starboard side and lay there, with water lapping at her rail.

Grabbing an ax, crewman Cray clambered forward, the deck steep beneath his feet. The first gust passed, and the *Clark* fought her way upright again. It was only the beginning.

Cray glanced at the deck. The hatch covers were off. Hours before, he and the others of the crew had been down in the hold, sweeping it out to get ready for the next cargo. There was no time to get the wooden hatches back on.

Another, stronger gust slammed into the *Clark*, now broadside to the wind. The young crewman tried to loosen the foresheet, but it was under pressure and jammed. With his ax, he began chopping at the sheets that held the sails trimmed for close-hauled sailing.

Too late. In the driving rain and hail, the *Clark* rolled down further on her leeward side. Chill waters surged into her open hatches. The young seaman threw down his ax and jumped to grab the windward rigging, his legs flying out from under him

Filled with water through her open hatches, the *Clark* sank bow first, since she carried her steel anchors, pins and heavy chain forward. She slid to the bottom and settled upright in the chill, dark depths of fresh water. Her masts were still in her, projecting upward toward the light. The tips reached 40 feet from the surface.

She snuggled into the silt that would preserve her intact and undisturbed. She was lost to the outside world for over 100 years.

A nearby vessel that had watched her go under sent a yawl boat to pick up the survivors. Only Cray and another crewman still lived. Lost forever in the depths were the captain, the mate and the passenger.

······················ ❀ ······················

It was on a raw day in November 1967, when a commercial fisherman aboard the *Dellie W.*, out of Menominee, Michigan, cussed, then threw the trawler into reverse. He gunned the diesel .

His nylon trawl net was entangled on the bottom off the northeast end of Chambers Island. After trying to free it by pulling and maneuvering,

Dick Garbowski cut the lead line and tied a buoy to the end, marking the location.

Disheartened with the loss of his valuable nets, he returned ashore and called an amateur diver to look at the tangled nets. Something had snagged them; maybe the diver, Frank Hoffmann, could untangle the nets without cutting them and bring them back.

It was worth a try. Hoffmann was a diving enthusiast who ran a bar and motel in Egg Harbor, Wisconsin, on the Door County Peninsula. He had done underwater searches. He also had an old boat he ran as a charter service for divers.

With temperatures in the 30s, the *Dellie W.* approached the bobbing markers where the nets had snagged. On the way out, the fishermen for the first time told Hoffman that they had made a sonar scan of the bottom area. They saw a ship down there.

It was an old one, since they saw masts, but they didn't much care. They wanted their $1,400 net back.

.... ❊ ....

Shivering in the cold, Hoffmann donned his wet suit, pulled on his double SCUBA tanks, flippers, and grabbed his old diving light, which sometimes didn't work. He also tied on two knives (one to use; one to lose), just in case of trouble. Nets can be dangerous entanglements to divers.

For safety, SCUBA divers go down in pairs. But on such a short notice, Frank Hoffmann couldn't get anyone to dive with him. He dove alone.

Jumping off the fishing boat, Hoffmann splashed into the chill waves and followed the lead line down. The water was murky, roiled by late fall waves. Visibility was only a few feet. At about 50 feet down, he switched on his diving light. That improved visibility to six feet.

At about 90 feet, something loomed ahead in the darkness. He couldn't see much in the feeble yellow light, but as he moved his beam around, he realized that he was looking at the undamaged front end of an old ship—an ancient wooden ship.

His battered diving lamp began to blink. He shook it, and in its wavering illumination, drifted forward. Time to go to work.

The net was wrapped around the bow in several places. Reaching for his diving knife, he found he had lost it, so he pulled out his spare. But as he worked one line free, he found that another section of net also had to be pulled free.

As he grabbed the net, his diving light went out. In the bottom's blackness, he yanked on the net and bounced up and down—surface waves were jousting with the net's buoys.

To his amazement, the jiggling turned his light back on and he saw that the nets were tangled in several places. He couldn't free the nets in a single dive.

Hoffmann glanced at his diving watch: his bottom time was up. He rose to the surface, watching the water grow brighter as he came out of the depths. By the time the *Dellie W.'s* crew hoisted him aboard, he was shivering but excited.

He had not retrieved their nets, but he had located what looked like every diver's dream—a virgin shipwreck.

.... ❀ ....

When he returned to his bar, Hoffmann called friends who were amateur SCUBA divers. Before he moved to Egg Harbor, Hoffmann had run a janitorial service in Chicago and was an active sport diver. His friends headed to Door County the following weekend, wondering what he had found.

He had only been down on the bottom a few minutes, in limited visibility, but he had done it again—found another wreck. The wreck was his. The fishermen didn't have an interest in an old ship; they just wanted their valuable net. Hoffmann worked out a deal with them so that any salvageable cargo aboard would go to the fishermen, but the ship would belong to Hoffmann.

Hoffman's friends hoped it was not a repeat of the *Jennybel*. A few years back, a commercial fishing boat also had wrapped its nets around an old vessel—much like the sunken ship Hoffmann had just been down on—that had sunk in Green Bay.

She was an old schooner, lying upright in about 95 feet of water, beside a deep trench. The old ship had sunk in 1881 while being towed from Death's Door. She had capsized and lay on the bottom still filled with cordwood.

Local fishermen had snagged valuable nets and wanted them cleared and brought up. Diving on the vessel, Hoffmann cleared the nets and later talked about raising her. She was, he exclaimed, an old schooner sitting upright with her hull intact and her masts still standing. Nobody had found an intact vessel like this before.

Word spread to rival divers, who made secret night dives on her and took off artifacts. One night, they attempted to raise her.

When Hoffman heard about it, he raced his boat out and screamed at the amateur salvagers to stop. They had towed a barge out atop the old schooner, fastened a single, heavy cable around the ship's bow and another around her stern. They joined these two looped cables at a single, central union.

When their crane lifted, the old schooner broke in half. Her hull snapped like a twig.

The broken old boat is still down at the bottom, stripped of anything of interest or value. Hoffman had lost his schooner—but learned a valuable lesson.

This time, Hoffmann swore everyone to secrecy. Once again, he was worried that other amateur divers might come in and loot the wreck for souvenirs, or even try to raise her. It was a free-for-all time in the 1960s, when there were no archeological laws in place to protect wrecks. Anyone could go down on a sunken vessel and "souvenir" it to bare bones.

It would be Hoffmann's wreck—so long as no one else knew about it.

.... ✣ ....

It was a chill and windy November 6 when the Garbowski trawler *Dellie W.* again headed out for the wreck site. Onboard were Hoffmann and several fellow divers to do a survey of the old boat and to free the net, tangled in several places on the old schooner.

With Huffman were Dick Boyd and his diving partner, Carl Poster, both from Madison. Hoffmann had already been down on an exploratory dive with Bud Brain, of Chicago, but had spent only a little bottom time on the wreck.

As Boyd and Poster descended, they were surprised by poor visibility of only three to four feet. By 50 feet of depth, all surface light was erased. The divers could only see what their dive lights illuminated – a small beam that penetrated a few feet into the black water.

"We saw nothing until we hit the deck at about 90 feet," Boyd recalled. Onboard the old vessel, he began to feel a chill coming over him. He knew what was happening: At that depth, his wet suit of foam neoprene had compressed to one-fourth of its original thickness, losing much of its insulating value and its positive buoyancy.

He shrugged it off, entranced. "We could sense that the wooden vessel was in remarkable condition," he said.

Leaving the descending line, the divers followed the rail toward the stern of the ship. The deck inside the rail was littered with blocks, pulleys and other sailing artifacts.

"Some distance back, toward the ship's midline," Boyd related, "we could make out a giant, post-like object projecting into the gloom. It dawned on us that a mast was still standing. The realization that we were exploring an intact sailing schooner complete with standing masts crystallized in our chilled brains."

When they swam over several cargo holds, they saw that the hatch covers were missing. Reaching the aft cabin, they peered in the companionway to see that the cabin was completely silted in. They could not get a good look at the entire boat because, at a depth of up to 110 feet, they were working in blackness penetrated only a few feet by the lights of their diving lamps. Their movements would stir up bottom silt, cutting what little visibility they had even more.

Checking out the fisherman's net, the divers saw it was wrapped around the schooner's windlass, forward bit post and mast pin rail. They began to make plans to free the net without cutting it and concluded that it would take several dives to free the entanglement. Their bottom time up, they ascended the line, taking a short decompression stop at 10 feet.

Back aboard the fishing trawler, the divers were jubilant. They had been on a schooner of exceptional interest and intact with both masts still standing.

She was a virgin wreck—and a boat of mystery.

Who was she? How old was she? They had not seen a name board or other form of identification, nor any clue as to its actual age.

But she was ancient.

November winds scoured the lake, kicking up big waves, and creating another problem. Secured to a dock in Egg Harbor, with no shelter from the pounding waves, the 50-ton Garbowski trawler *Dellie W.* broke loose from her mooring lines and ran aground.

Diver Bernie Bloom recalls Hoffmann "running around like a crazy man," trying to make a rescue effort. "Frank tried to take his small boat out to pull the *Dellie W.* off the beach. The engine roared, the boat took up the strain, but the only thing Hoffman did was tear the Sampson post off his boat."

The *Dellie W.* rolled over on her side with her starboard deck down in the water. Waves pounded against her thick steel hull.

It took three big diesel-powered fishing trawlers to drag the *Dellie W.* free. But the big trawler needed repairs; their dive boat was out of commission for the rest of the diving season.

The divers were running out of luck.

.... ❀ ....

Hoffmann took his 27-foot powerboat, *Sea Witch*, to the dive site. But as Bernie Bloom recalls, "she was a wooden junker that had tin covering her bottom. She leaked."

It was a ride to the dive site he'd always remember. "As we motored out, the weather was cold, foggy and nasty." It was late in the season.

They planned to make two dives. On the first dive, they worked to clear the net, but without a lot of success. They found that the nets were wound around the bow section, snagged hard into the bowsprit, anchors and catheads.

"It was a downright treacherous job," Dick Boyd recalled. "The trawler had attempted to pull the net free and the nets had stretched across the ship's bow and her forward fixtures." Taut as banjo strings, they could whip outward or upward with great force when the divers tried to cut them free. The result could be deadly.

After they spent their 15 minutes on the bottom, they ascended to end their first dive session.

The divers had to wait out their full decompression time before doing their second dive, so they boated over to Menominee for lunch. They dropped off one diver to return home.

As they motored back to the dive site, the temperature had dropped to just above freezing. By 4 p.m., it was growing dark and they couldn't find their markers.

"By this time, it was blustery and snowing," Bloom recalls. The infamous Gales of November had descended.

As the light faded, they had about given up when Bloom saw the marker bobbing in the chill waves. "I thought of keeping my mouth shut," he said. Instead, he called out, "Here it is."

They tied off their boat to the marker, got into their cold, wet diving suits, and all three—Hoffman, Bud Brain and Bloom – went down in their SCUBA gear.

"It was a dumb thing to do, to leave the boat unattended," Bloom later recalled. "But we were in a state of high excitement."

In the darkness pierced only by their dive lights, they descended the mast onto the sunken ship.

"Fear was something you got used to," Bernie Bloom said. "You went down, down in the dark, and you couldn't see anything. *Bang!* There's a little adrenalin jolt as you see something in front of you. You reach out and touch it—your ship. You are home."

In the flickering light of their lamps, they leveled out a few feet above the deck and began moving to the cabin. "Swim fast and you run right into it, because you can only see a few feet. But you get used to it."

A plank to port side was hanging loose, and the young diver pulled it free. Inside lay the ship's galley, and, he saw a pestle and a wooden board and a hunk of soap, still intact. Bloom grabbed the soap as a souvenir.

They also swam over the stern, looking for a name board, but couldn't find any identification. The ship was still a mystery.

Their bottom time was up. They swam back to the mainmast and ascended. At its tip, where they had tied a line to their marker buoy, they went up to the surface.

By the time they poked their heads above water, it was dark and snowing. The waves were growing, but their boat was still there, bobbing with its nose to the storm.

"It was a hell of a ride back, dark and snowing," Bloom recalls. "And if our compass had gone out, we'd still be out there circling."

They didn't bother to get out of their wet suits; they were chilled to the bone. Bloom recalls sleeping in front of a fireplace, shivering but never getting warm, and in some stage of hypothermia.

"But we did a lot of that in those days," he said.

One thing was clear: The diving season was over for the year.

························ ✺ ·····················

During the winter, Hoffmann got official salvage rights to the old vessel. He alone owned it. He vowed to protect it from marauding amateur divers who, he feared, would "souvenir" the unprotected vessel bare.

His amateur diving group, enraptured by the lost schooner, was composed of divers from Chicago, Green Bay, and around southern Illinois and central Wisconsin. All drove over to dive. They paid their own expenses and worked for free.

Hoffman paid for equipment and the operation of his leaky old boats, no mean feat for a small-time saloonkeeper. Costs were mounting; Hoffmann had discovered an underwater archeological treasure but was facing a financial disaster.

In winter meetings, the divers began to plan what they wanted to do with the sunken boat. Everyone wanted to "keep it all intact, and not strip it."

It was the dream every diver hoped for—a virgin wreck undamaged and untouched, and looking like she could almost sail away on her own bottom. The divers felt privileged to dive on a pristine vessel; they were in awe of her.

They were lucky, too. She was preserved because she had gone down in fresh water. Old ships in saltwater don't last long underwater because their metal fittings rust away, and their wood gets devoured by wood-eating worms. The ships collapse inward upon themselves in little more than a half-century.

But in freshwater depths, the cold and the lack of salt and oxygen allow boats to remain undamaged for a long time.

Whoever she was, she was a unique old boat and beautiful. She had captured their imaginations and their hearts.

They were determined to salvage her, somehow.

························ ✺ ·····················

The next spring, as soon as the ice was off Green Bay, the divers went out to their dive site. Confounded, looked around for their buoys. They were missing.

Storms during the winter had blown away their markers—they had lost her.

Undaunted, they spent days locating the wreck and putting in new, more substantial markers.

Sliding down the lines, the divers probed the wreck. It amazed them to find that the hull seemed solid and well preserved. It was intact, except for some of the booms and rigging that were missing, but the divers figured they had to be around somewhere in the silt. The cargo holds, open to view, were filled with mud.

The ship's wheel had a curious canvas covering. When the divers touched it, the fabric covering over the spokes disintegrated. They decided it was a safety measure. By covering the wheel's spokes with canvas, a helmsman would not break an arm or a wrist during heavy weather.

When divers swam around, their movements stirred up bottom silt. Visibility was so poor, Hoffmann said, "we could hold a diving light against our face masks and barely make out the dim glow of the filament inside."

They needed some kind of suction device to clean out the silt inside the cabin and the holds. Because the amateur divers had no funds to buy this equipment, they began experimenting with various makeshift systems they could put together. Early efforts only roiled up the silt.

After burning up several small pumps, they hadn't even cleared out the small cabin. They needed a bigger device and Hoffmann scrounged up an old five-inch fire pump that the village of Egg Harbor had used. They'd gotten it as Army Surplus.

With a bigger pump, they needed a bigger boat.

Hoffmann's two small wooden boats wouldn't do, since they often were dangerously overloaded with crew, pumps, diving gear and equipment. Hoffmann's 27-foot *Sea Witch* and 34-foot *Sea Ranger* were old and leaky.

The divers called them three-man boats: One to pilot, one to keep the machinery running, and one to bail. They weren't kidding.

.... ❖ ....

Harold Derusha, of Marinette Marine Corporation, closely followed the amateur divers' problems. He stepped in: "Come and get the barge," he said.

It amazed everyone. Derusha had just offered the divers the loan of his World War II-era landing craft, *Cleo's Barge*, a 56-foot vessel that would hold the big new pump and its engine.

"It had twin diesels. A cabin. It was big," Bloom said. "And best of all, it had heat."

Derusha told them that when they needed diesel fuel, just to stop by his business and fill up.

It was an incredible offer. The amateur divers now had a big craft and all the fuel they wanted.

.... ❀ ....

But after they mounted their fire pump on *Cleo's Barge*, they had to figure out how to get their giant suction device working. They had to clear out more than a century of silt and mud from the old vessel. The job was enormous: they had to move about 20,000 cubic feet of mud.

They tied an aluminum pipe to the sunken schooner's upright mast. To this they attached flexible hoses, at the top, to *Cleo*, and, from the bottom, to the divers. In that way, when *Cleo* left the diving site for the night, they could disconnect the flexible tube and leave the underwater gear in place, ready to hook up the next day. Below, the divers would be ready to pick up their flexible hose from where they left it the day before. It was a good system.

They added two screens, one at the intake on the wreck, and, another at the surface. That way they would not lose any artifact that might get sucked up.

To work the new suction device, one diver remained at the bottom, moving the intake over the silt to suck it up. In the close confines of the cabin or the hold, only one diver could work at a time. He labored alone in silt and blackness, often losing his sense of direction. It was hard, mean work; a challenge for the bravest of divers.

"You went into the hold," Bloom recalls, "and wrapped your legs around the pipe."

The diver held the suction head between his legs and leaned out, scooping mud with both arms toward the wire screen at the end of the hose. When the diver was scooping in the cabin's darkness, he could only feel the artifacts as they came toward the power head. The diver then picked these out and set them outside on the deck, only a few feet away.

A diver faced the possibility that the excavation might collapse over him like an underwater grave, leaving him alone and trapped under tons of mud. With silt and debris billowing about, there was also possibility that a diver's regulator might clog up. Or, the big suction hose might tear out of his grasp, flogging back and forth and injuring the diver.

It took nerves.

Bloom shrugged off the dangers: "I once encountered a mudslide," he said, "because the tool and I dug a tunnel that collapsed on me." But it didn't prevent him from continuing. "The water with the mud kept the mud fluid and not in a dangerous situation," he said. "You just dug your way back out."

After a while, they turned their diving lights off. "It saved the battery, and, besides it was so dark you couldn't see anything anyway," Bloom recalls.

The amateur divers started making their own underwater lights by wiring an automotive sealed beam spotlight ("good to a depth of 200 feet") to a battery and stuffing that in a fiberglass case.

Here the divers divided into two distinct technology camps: some preferred to hang their underwater lamps with straps to their wrists. Others fastened them to a hockey helmet, so that wherever their head turned they'd have light.

.... ※ ....

The extreme depths and the chill 30- to 40-degree waters at the bottom took their toll. Their foam neoprene suits in these depths compressed, taking away part of the suit's normal heat-retaining insulation, making the divers chill. The divers learned to work in 20-minute shifts. They found that 20 minutes on the bottom would allow them to surface without having to decompress in stages ascending. Divers often came up shivering from the bottom cold.

It took a monumental amount of work to clear out the cabin, and, after that, the forepeak and the holds. They removed about ten tons of mud and silt from inside the old vessel. Up came artifacts, including plates, dishes, silverware, some items of leather objects and tools.

From the silted galley, they recovered several porcelain China pieces. Emblems on the bottoms dated them back to the early 1860s, showing that the vessel was pre-Civil War.

"This discovery," Dick Boyd recalls, "generated great public and media interest and was the catalyst for the intense media scrutiny that then began to follow the project."

Besides the china, the divers found some remarkable artifacts. "In one case, a duck with its flesh still in place was found within the silt," Boyd said. "This bird was a deep-diving species, so we assumed that it had gotten trapped within the hull long after it sank. Upon closer inspection, it became clear that the creature's head had been cut off and its feathers had been plucked and singed. It had been prepared for cooking." The frigid environment had preserved its flesh intact for 105 years.

At about the time the discoveries were being made, the divers made a tentative identification of the boat they were diving on and learned about the loss of life during the *Alvin Clark's* sinking. Three victims were never recovered.

"After seeing the preserved, fleshy duck," Boyd recalls, "the divers working inside the ship in total darkness became very anxious whenever they encountered any soft mass."

The divers discovered another unique artifact: a simple earthenware jar of homemade cheese. It was common foodstuff aboard sailing vessels and called "crock cheese."

When the silt was removed, Boyd said, "the cheese proved unspoiled and edible." In fact, when the cheese was examined at the University of Wisconsin, the bacterium used to produce the curd was still recoverable in a viable state. After they brought it up, several adventurous divers tasted a bit of the cheese from this large crock.

"It wasn't very good," Boyd said. "However, I'm told that sailor's Crock Cheese was pretty bad even when it was freshly made."

They sent this cheese to the Kraft's Food Museum in Philadelphia, where it lives in all its glory as the world's oldest edible cheese—another marvel from the *Mystery Ship*.

.... ❀ ....

They were scraping by. Hoffmann joked that their diving work was patched together by Christian Brothers brandy and carpet tape. The brandy was for the divers coming up from the chilled waters; the carpet tape was to tape up holes in the divers' suits. It also patched other things, including holes in the flexible suction tubes.

Undaunted, they decided to try to raise her.

On September 24, 1968, they began boring underneath the wreck. They decided that her hull was in good enough shape to raise, and besides, they'd excavated most of the mud from the inside of the ship. Now all they had to do was bore a small hole through the mud all the way under the vessel and out the other side.

They found a way to reverse the engine and use the former suction head as a power blower with 200 pounds of pressure. Marinette Marine built them a special water jet cutting head—an inch and a half diameter pipe with a curved radius—with side pressure vents to neutralize the blast.

The plan was to insert the water jet head down into the clay and silt to follow the hull's curvature, but there was a lot of pressure. Bloom said the unit moved him around underwater, so they got the biggest diver, Gary Means, to wrestle the cutting tool.

Figuring out how to get the holes straight was a special problem. Means would go to his diving station, marked out ahead of time. Bloom would swim straight out over the deck and when he could see Means' light, he'd cut 90 degrees to the ship's keel.

The big engine on *Cleo* threw 200 pounds of pressure into the water jet. Means shoved it into the mud and it dug like crazy until it popped out on the other side—"like a blowtorch through butter," Bloom said.

They put a line on the head, and when they pulled it back out—they had a line under the keel. Bloom said: "It worked beautiful."

Late in the season, the lake was acting up with large swells. Snow was on the way. Several times they had to postpone dives because the barge was moving so much that it tossed the hose about, making it impossible for the divers to work. They dug seven holes—one twice, because it got crooked.

The weather was freezing, and waves were running up to five feet. But they had few days left, so divers went down to attach lifting cables to the under-hull slings. The divers did one or two at a time, leaving the cables fall back to the deck. They were ready for final hookup.

Divers removed everything from the hull that would interfere with her raising, including anchors, loose chain and fittings. They also brought up more artifacts, including the captain's writing desk, a brass locket, clay pipes, a clock, an oil lamp and a wallet.

They had the wreck ready for lifting.

.... ❈ ....

Money was running out. Hoffmann had borrowed heavily, and these funds were used up. Over the winter, Hoffmann tried to launch a fund raising. Though the diving group got great publicity, they got very little cash. Marinette Marine contributed some money.

Hoffmann took out a second mortgage on his bar and motel. He bought gear and supplies on his credit cards.

He hoped for financial success when and if the *Clark* could be raised. It would be a one-of-a-kind vessel, brought back from the deep— a sure-fire tourist attraction.

In reality he was going broke.

The strain began to show. He intended to bring the *Clark* to Door County, where the beautiful area's booming tourist trade might provide a base for financial support.

After a series of combative disagreements, Hoffmann turned his back on the tourism-rich peninsula where he had his bar. He looked instead to the opposite side of Green Bay. Though the tourist trade was thinner on this side of the lake—much, much thinner—Hoffmann still hoped that his fantastic find could be put on display to pay its own way.

.... ❈ ....

On June 1969, the diving season opened by blowing so hard that the Cleo's anchor line snapped. The divers had to return to shore.

The next day, they anchored over the wreck and began pumping silt again. The divers began to collect any artifacts that had fallen around the wreck site and to get the old schooner ready to be raised. That meant removing the masts.

"But who the hell knew how to take the masts out of a hundred-year-old boat?" Bloom recalled. "They sit in a hole in the keel, and wedged into the deck, with the wedges tapering in both directions."

He added, "A beautiful fit. And swelled in after being down that long."

Their first attempt was to pry out the wedges from the topside deck, but they couldn't budge the water-swollen wood. Next, they went below into the hold and tried to push the wedges up from the underside. The result was that they broke two jacks, each with a five-ton capacity.

Undaunted, they built a special jack atop an adjustable base made by placing three pipes with decreasing diameter inside each other. This formed a strong pedestal, atop which they mounted a ten-ton hydraulic ram. It took two divers to take this device below decks, place the base against the ship's keel, and jack up the ram to push the wedges up and out.

They did all the work in the confined, silty darkness of the hold. It was, as Boyd later recalled, "a daunting endeavor." But it worked.

Once they got the wedges out, they still had to figure out how to raise the masts. They also had to figure out how to raise the 220-ton schooner.

It seemed impossible. They first considered air bags, but the divers soon discarded the concept since they needed to control the rate of ascent. Once the hull broke loose from the bottom, the air bags could come up too fast and injure a diver. Or their velocity from 110 feet could be too uneven or too great, allowing the schooner to wobble, break out of the slings, or, even to cause damage to surface vessels.

They settled on old-fashioned hand-powered winches to raise the boat at the rate they wanted. It would give them great control.

Marionette Marine donated a lift barge that would be anchored in place atop the *Clark*. On each side of the barge, workers welded powerful, if cumbersome, hand-powered winches. Bloom recalls: "Jim DeRusha, the son of the owner of Marinette Marine and a Naval Architect, told us what and how to do it."

To get ready for the lift, they had to raise the masts. Divers went down to the old schooner and tied loops of line around each mast. A crane mounted on a Gallagher Marine construction barge took up the strain. Its diesel engine roaring, up came the old masts with no problems.

After being underwater for over 105 years, the masts were in excellent condition. It was a good omen.

·················· ✼ ··················

At 4 a.m. Wednesday, July 23, in the pre-dawn hours, it was dark on the water. They went ahead, rather than wait. Since the divers were working in darkness anyway on the bottom, there was no reason to hold off the long-awaited project for daylight hours.

The hull was sitting in about 10 feet of mud, so divers began sluicing mud from the low side of the hull with the water jet. Other divers fitted slings to the lifting cables.

They began cranking the hand-powered winches on the *Clark's* low side, canted to starboard. The barge squatted down in the water about eight inches. They worried about the strain, but the cables held.

Twelve men cranked harder and the barge sank another four inches. Then, it bobbed up six inches.

"The rolling action broke the suction on the bottom," Bloom said. The wreck was free of the mud and suspended beneath the barges in her slings.

It took 100 turns on a single winch to raise the wreck five inches. A crew could last only about 100 turns on a single winch before another crew took up the job.

Boaters who came out for a look at the salvage operation found themselves welcomed on board. They also were invited to take a turn at the four winches. "We exhausted everyone who came along," Bloom said.

The cumbersome hand-powered winches were slow, but they gave the divers total control of their lift.

By 3 p.m., the wreck was within 60 feet of the surface. A storm approached, and the crew took up the barge's anchors and began moving the boat toward shore. Volunteers cranked to raise the *Clark*—they didn't want to lose her now.

The squall hit, with high winds and heavy rain, but dissipated in about half an hour. The schooner stayed in place.

As they moved toward shore, the *Clark* dragged bottom in about 45 feet of water. The day's effort was over. *Cleo's Barge* set her anchors. The divers were exhausted.

They had worked nonstop for two days.

.... ❈ ....

The next day, they brought her upriver to Marinette Marine. All the time, the divers continued cranking the ship up, watching.

There was a stirring in the water.

Ahead of the barge, the schooner's bowsprit broke water—the first time in 105 years that the old schooner had come back to the surface.

Crowds lining the river's banks cheered. Ecstatic, the divers clapped each other on the back.

At Marinette Marine, two large cranes on barges and two on shore took over the job and continued to lift the old vessel. She broke surface, decks awash but still intact. Pumps whirred to drive water out; the divers clambered aboard and grabbed buckets to remove the last of the bottom mud inside her.

Hoffman and his crew stood in open-eyed admiration. Though he and his divers had been diving for years in the dark depths, they now saw for the first time the entire ship.

"We were amazed as much as anyone else," he said.

They had another surprise: the *Clark* floated on her own bottom. The divers discovered her seams were still tight and her caulking still in place after more than a century underwater.

It was a joyous, momentous, and historic moment. The effort had taken two years and 3,000 dives, but the *Alvin Clark* was afloat again. Never had a vessel like this, in mint condition and floating on her own, come up intact from the deep. It was an almost miraculous rising under incredible conditions and hardships, and it was all done, with great courage and resourcefulness, by a few dedicated American sport divers. ☸

12

The day Superior went wild

★★★

The storm of the century catches a small boat

MY VHF RADIO'S NOAA WEATHER BROADCAST assured me that today, July 4, 1999, would be the hottest day of the year There would be the possibilities of thunderstorms, but only later in the day. So far, so good.

I tapped my barometer, noticing the needle rise just a twitch to show fair weather. A rising barometer. Double good.

Out on Grand Portage Bay, cotton-candy fog wrapped a small island. To the north, a wreath of the gray stuff hid an historic eighteenth century fort. Thick fog hung across the Sawtooth Mountains.

Peeking out of the clouds was a burning yellow orb. The sun.

I walked over a plank past a rusting barge and into the marina office. "Oh, the fog will burn off," the manager advised me. "I'd go."

On Lake Superior, my 20-foot homemade boat *Persistence* seemed held aloft on the transparent inland sea. We ducked in and out of spectral fog banks. I was running my two-cycle outboard, with my sails uncovered, ready to hoist. Entering the chill fog banks was like entering a tomb: cold and damp. I was getting chilled despite my layers of thermal underwear, polar fleece and wool socks.

It was hard to remember that this was the 4th of July.

Persistence's 5 h.p Nissan outboard chortled at about a third throttle on the start of my latest solo adventure on Lake Superior. I planned to sail into what would be the world's largest freshwater conservation area along

Superior's Canadian north shore. It was an area of 11,000 square kilometers, stretching from Sleeping Giant Mountain to the Slate Islands.

················· ✾ ·················

I expected an easy run across the Canadian / U.S. border. My destination was a small island guarding the mouth of Thunder Bay.

I had dogged shut all hatches and took care to center my boat's weight. All the gear, extra water, food cans and sleeping bags I could move was out of the boat's ends and lashed to the centerboard trunk.

I was ready for mighty Superior. This was not my first dance on the world's largest freshwater lake. I had learned to be wary.

················· ✾ ·················

Out of nowhere, a monster jumped over the mountains, gripped my mast and swung the boat from side to side. A wall of wind slammed through the shrouds, beginning with a low moan, then moved to a howl and to a high-pitched shriek.

My boat bucked out of control, slewing to one side as I tried to get her bow downwind—the classic heavy weather storm tactic.

The wind had us in its grip, shoving Persistence faster and faster. My boat nosed into a wave. Her bow went down as she caught blue water, her stern rose. I was in a pitch pole.

I was lofted into the air and tossed through the hatch into the cabin. I flew headfirst, with feet above my head. A sharp, stabbing pain hit my right side. Then the pain hit my head.

When I came to a few seconds later, I was dizzy and disoriented. I looked up and I saw my alarm clock fly from one side of my cabin to the another. It came to rest beside the starboard portlight. But something was wrong: I shook my head to clear it; my starboard portlight had turned green. A beautiful green. I admired the green for a moment.

Whoa! My boat's entire side was underwater.

Persistence seemed to teeter for a small eternity, balancing on its side. It nearly turned over. I saw myself trapped below, splashing about in icy waters, and then having to swim down to get out.

Wham. The boat lurched again. Something fell on me—a duffle of foul weather clothing—followed by bags of groceries and a plastic carton. The port side had emptied its contents on me.

The wind screamed like a banshee. I saw water slosh up through the open centerboard case. From behind me, my engine was howling—its propeller out of the water.

It took several bewildered seconds before I realized what had happened. The winds had caught us, thrown us forward. We went faster and faster, until we stopped. The bow stuffed itself in a wave. The stern flew up, the bow dug in. I'd been dumped forward, up through an open hatch, and down into the cabin. I lay dazed in the starboard quarter berth, with my feet over my head.

My mind sent out little queries. I wriggled one ankle, then the other. Did I break anything? No, but I hurt a lot in a lot of places.

I pulled myself up. In the cockpit, rain like lead drops pelted my face. Wind roared as I faced my old enemy. The lake was blasted by terrible gusts. Long contrails of mist snaked across the water like icy whips.

My boat teetered on its side, reeling with every gust. The starboard mast spreader dipped into the water, rose a little. Then it hung a few feet above the water.

Hand over hand, I worked my way back to the transom.

My hand closed in a death grip on the tiller.

Another huge gust tore into us. I felt us going down further.

No! I threw myself overboard. I ended up just over the windward lifelines, trying to use my weight to lever the boat down. But the storm was too strong: the boat remained on its side. My weight made no difference.

After an eternity, the mast soared upright. The hull descended with a mighty splash. With a growling noise, the propeller bit into solid water and the engine's racing stopped. I could feel the rudder blade slice back beneath the waves.

Nothing broken. I had control again.

We picked up speed as *Persistence* headed downwind—the classic heavy weather maneuver. Now we were taking the wild gusts on the transom instead of our vulnerable beam.

That didn't seem to help a lot. In the wind's gusts, the mast still seemed to want to squirrel down into the water.

I couldn't see too well, since my glasses were misted over. I was in a world of hurt, with no place to run to, no place to hide, and nobody to help me.

Another violent gust flattened us. As the boat laid over, I heard a "ping" noise. Something had snapped.

I saw the furled mainsail break loose from its shock chords. The wind's icy fingers began to shove it up the mast. The big sail reared a third of the way up, flapping, rattling and catching the wind.

My heart pounded. We were already on the edge of capsizing. I could not leave the helm.

⁂

We ran into the raging lake.

I felt the wind letting up a little. I steeled myself. Timing the gusts, I shoved the tiller over hard—and hung on. *Persistence* did a dangerous dip to leeward and hung down on her lee rail. Dark waters rushed up.

The sail rattled and whipped on the mast. But we turned.

One hand on the tiller, I gave the engine full throttle and locked it there. Power. I had to have more power in the teeth of the storm.

The five horsepower outboard bellowed and dug in. Sometimes the prop was in the water; sometimes out. The little Nissan screamed.

But we were gaining.

⁂

I wiped my glasses with my fingers to clear them. Ahead lay a row of rocky pinnacles, slashed with waves and spray. They stretched from the northeastern edge of Spar Island into the lake. In the distance, through the rain, I could make out a gray blob. It had to be Thompson Island. My haven.

Persistence staggered, her speed knocked down. Her rail dipped low into the water. I edged my upper body over the port side, my leg locked around the traveler beam, one arm around a winch. I reached for my NOAA chart and a cruising guidebook, which I had jammed to one side of my gas tank. Both were soaked; ink was running off the chart where I had pre-marked my course. I dared not let the wind get these. They were my only guides to the wilderness ahead.

I approached the island. But where was the harbor? I tried to find a solution. If I ran all the way alongside the island to its tip, I'd come across the hidden harbor. No problemo.

.... ❈ ....

I saw a dark blue line etched on the water. It was moving—rushing toward me. That much blue on the water meant only one thing: wind. Tons of it.

Howling, the storm switched from the west, veering to catch me again. The first blasts shook my boat. The tiller twisted in my hand as my boat bucked and took a dive to starboard. We were down on our beam ends, cabin side going under, mast spreaders dipping in the water. Icy waves climbed the side of my boat, splashing into the cockpit.

We neared a dangerous place—a gap between the land and a small island. A wave flung spray high into the air. I saw what lay beneath: reefs.

On the horizon appeared something green. The island? I took a deep breath. Adrenalin surging, I charged the gap with the engine cranked up to full maximum.

I lost control. In a heart-stopping moment, we careened toward the islet's foam-lashed reefs. I swore, prayed, steered and shifted my weight round.

I circled. Time to try again. This time, I went further east, letting the tiny islet take the blast of the waves and wind. I braced myself. I squeezed the throttle hard to be certain I had every ounce of power the engine could give me.

We charged—bouncing, careening, splashing. We were through the gap.

I was facing huge, square rollers—the worst waves I'd fought all day.

My speeding bow speared into the first oncoming tower; the impact shook the boat. The bow disappeared, but the water kept coming over the cabin top and hit me in the chest. I groaned at the chill. We climbed the wave, teetering at the top. For the first time, I could see what lay ahead.

I had made a big mistake.

That distinctive island ahead of me was none other than Pie Island. This was not the hidden harbor.

I timed the waves. On the back of one of the steep chargers, I turned the little boat around. We were flying back now, surfing the waves. Ahead, the gap loomed.

Then we were through. I was growing exhausted. My reactions were slowing; I couldn't think. Icy water doused me; I was shivering, cold to my body core.

Rocky slopes rushed close by my speeding boat. Beyond one crag, I saw something shining. Up high, above the trees.

They were the tips of sailboat masts.

Roaring closer, I saw that on one side of the boat was a high outcrop of rock, and on the other, a green, spruce-covered hill. In between, a blue water channel opened up. It was blessed, beautiful Thomson cove. I had arrived.

I was tying up when I heard my VHF boom: "Calling the sailboat *Persistence*."

It was the Thunder Bay Coast Guard. I realized that I was long overdue on my schedule. They were ready to start a search-and-rescue mission. I had not heard them calling when I was in the cockpit, surrounded by the noise of the storm, flapping sail, and engine.

"Sorry," I keyed my mike. "But I've been little busy." ☸

13

The old shipwright from Thunder Bay

---***---

A man wise in the old ways of boats and the inland sea

SHE HAD TALL WOODEN MASTS, sails lashed the old way to her booms, and a long wooden bowsprit—something out of another era. I had been told about her and the single-hander who sailed her. Some said he was a dreamer, a man who built wooden boats the old way and sailed them alone on Superior's chilly waters.

With his white beard and dark clothing, he was well known to the waterfront community as a perpetual wanderer upon the lake. With fall in the air, he had returned.

The *Carioca* was now in Prince Albert Marina in Thunder Bay, Ontario, in the shadows of the Sleeping Giant.

Albert Leon was seated in the cockpit of his old sloop, warming himself in the late afternoon sun. He stared at what he saw on the horizon. Perhaps he saw something I did not; perhaps he heard something I could not hear.

I began to introduce myself, but he waved his hand. "I know who you are." He smiled.

"We're sinking," he told me. He invited me on board. I accepted.

He had sailed to one of his favorite places on Superior, the Slate Islands along the north Canadian shore, but had hit a reef. "I thought I had run out of luck."

He had hit hard but a few large waves came along and boosted

Carioca from one rock to another. "We bounced a while," he told me. "They just shoved me off."

The old wooden boat bounced sideways across reefs in high winds and seas. The old man got through the ordeal with a leaking boat. But still afloat.

I stole a glance below. Yes. Water gurgled in the floorboards.

He could not see the source of the leak, but he thought it was under some planking. He would know since he built the boat himself. He picked out every plank.

"The shock pushed the frames upward and the damage may swell up or realign itself. I've had that happen before."

Albert was the shipwright at Old Fort William, near Thunder Bay, Ontario. The old fur fort's stockade and buildings stood at Pointe de Meuron, along the ancient Voyageur's route up the Kaministrikwia River from Lake Superior. Fur trappers and explorers portaged and paddled on this "fur highway" as far north as the Arctic Ice and as far west as the Pacific Ocean.

In the fort's boat shop, he specialized in old Lake Superior craft. He researched original documents for old sailing vessels, drew up his own plans, found his own wood in the north woods, and built them with hand tools as ancient as 150 years old. He came to appreciate hand tools.

"The adz is very efficient. I got so I did everything with it including sharpening my pencil. You can cut curves, cut straight, reduce a board by a sixteenth of an inch, or take off an inch at a whack. It's my favorite tool and I've still got both legs."

I straightened up. "What?"

"I've got both legs because I've avoided using the broadax. The head of it weighs three times as much as an adz and your leg must be on the same side you're chopping. With an adz, you straddle a log and if the head slips, it just slips between your legs. I've found that with a chalk line and an adz, I can make a round pole, or taper it. We even made our masts that way."

For materials, he scoured the nearby woods for white pine, spruce, birch, ash and elm. He prized Tamarack for crooks and ribs. Sometimes, Albert sent his students into the forests with a pattern to find a crook that matched.

"How old are your tools?"

"Anywhere from 80 to 150 years," he said. "On some of them, the handgrip is so small I can only get two fingers in them."

He explained: "Smaller men. I've got one four-foot jack plane with a hole in it, not a handle, and when I use it, one of my fingers just sticks out. The plane must have weighed as much as the man using it."

I always imagined the men who braved the wilderness were hearty giants. He shook his head. He told me that the original Voyageurs who came here were only a little over five feet tall.

He saw my surprise, adding: "Yes, but they were muscular. They had to be. Their work would either make a person muscular or dead. I believe they were stronger than we are. Think of the Voyageurs carrying two and three 90- pound packs on the Grand Portage. It is nine miles uphill over a very rocky trail."

"Why did they carry so much?"

"They had a choice. Each Voyageur had to carry so many packs up the trail. They could either carry one pack and make two or three trips, or carry all the packs at once, then rest. A lot of the Voyageurs carried three packs, each weighing 90 pounds.

He paused. "If you can get anyone these days even six feet tall to carry a 90-pound pack up that portage they wouldn't speak for weeks – they'd be in a state of total collapse."

.... ❈ ....

Since he was a shipwright, I asked him about the birchbark canoe—a legendary basket of cedar, spruce and birchbark, ultralight for carrying through the woods yet strong enough to brave the waves of Lake Superior. It had no metal fastenings.

He told me that the fort built two or three of them each season. He smiled: "I never had a birch bark canoe that didn't leak. They leaked in the old days too," he said.

"The Indian used to load his canoe properly, which is to say, very little. But the Voyageurs overloaded them, putting two-and-a-half tons in a 26-footer and four tons in a 36-footer. Birch was never designed by nature for anything that heavy.

"In winter, they used to sink the canoes in rivers so they would not dry out. They'd fill them full of rocks and sink them under water. When they'd take them out in the spring, they were just like when they were put in. If you hung them up on stands from fall to spring, all the cedar lining and the ribs would just fall out of the boat, since there's nothing holding them in. They are not tied or sewed, just tucked in. It's the water always leaking in that kept the canoes swelled up and tight."

"How well did they handle?"

"The steering was done from the bow and the helmsman was an expert. He was paid almost twice as much as the standard paddler. That's because if he made a mistake, good-bye canoe and most of the crew, since few of them could swim. With a full load, canoes don't turn at all well. You get the feeling you're on a hand car. You're trying to turn, but the canoe wants to stay on the track and go straight ahead."

He continued: "I never get over how strong they were. They came from the farm. Think about it: in spring, they planted their crops and they had very little to do till harvest. So, they signed on with a company to go a couple thousand miles into the wilderness. They were absolutely at the mercy of their employers and the work was hard and dangerous. Some came back home with hernias and ruptures, which made them useless.

"How did farmers get to be so good with canoes?"

"You remember that farms were sited up the Saint Lawrence River. No farming was done inland since there were no roads.

"How long did they stay Voyageurs?"

"Records show that only one in seven signed up for a second year. Think about that. One in seven."

We sat talking on the slowly sinking sailboat. From time to time, he checked the bilge and so did I. The creeping water was visible and the sight of it gave me a shudder. But I was having an enjoyable time; I did not want to get off the boat.

.... ✿ ....

I leaned back in the cockpit, feeling the sun on my shoulders and a gentle wind on my face. I glanced up: I saw something in the mists beyond the harbor. This was where the old shipwright had been looking. There was something shining, white—maybe a sailboat—and then it was gone. I was not even certain I had even seen it.

A scene in the movie, *Jeremiah Johnson*, flashed through my mind. Two mountain men sit high above the snowline, looking out into the distance. They had been in the mountains a long time; one of them—I think it was Robert Redford—asks what season of the year it was—as casually as if he had asked for the time.

"Sorry, Pilgrim," the other answers. He guesses it might be April, maybe May, but he does not care. And so, they sit staring out at nothing in particular, waiting, lost like pilgrims in a world that they had been caught up in and did not want to leave.

It was that way for me.

The boat might sink. It might not. I finished my beer and was about to leave when I turned to ask him if there was anything I could do. *Persistence* was berthed where I could see his boat. He looked at the horizon again, then shrugged his shoulders.

"Take a bearing from time to time on my masts and the stars," he said. "And if my masts aren't up there, you know I am in trouble"

"Sure enough," I said.

As I walked away, I thought I heard the word, Pilgrim, uttered, somewhere.

··················· ❀ ···················

Years later, *Persistence* and I ran aground on some reefs on the north shore. After rescuers pulled me off with their boat, we talked. They were from Thunder Bay, near the old fur fort. I inquired about Albert Leon. They told me he died a few years earlier.

"We were friends and we carried out his last wishes. We took his ashes out in our boat to his favorite place, the Slate Islands," they told me. "You know he always wanted to come back as a seagull."

The Slates? A seagull? Shoving off from Rossport, I pointed my sailboat southeasterly. As I sailed closer, I saw blue peaks emerge out of the water like something out of the movie, *South Pacific*. The Slates were unusual and had been formed millions of years ago by meteorites striking the earth. I could see Albert's attraction.

Guided by GPS, I entered a center channel, with Lampton Cove as my intended harbor for the night. After overshooting my GPS landmark, I turned my boat around, and, with some misgivings, nudged my bow into what looked like a crack in some rocks. That was the entryway, all right. Once again, the magic of the shoreline opened to me.

I watched my depth sounder. The steep rocky shores lead down to the water's edge. I followed the curve of the island until I emerged in water about 10 to 12 feet deep. It was so clear I felt I was like I was flying my boat over air.

At the base of a rocky outcropping, I came across a small wooden dock. I had planned to anchor in the cove, but the dock was just long enough for my little sailboat. Perfect.

Home for the night in Lampton Cove, I unclipped my safety harness, and, stepped ashore to explore the tiny island. It felt good to stretch my sea legs.

On the far shore, I saw a movement. A large animal with a rack of antlers and huge hooves drifted to the water's edge. It was a woodland caribou gathering his evening meal These islands are the furthest south locations of the great beasts of the Arctic Circle. The thought came to me once again that these islands were a special place. A kind of paradise.

I stood there a moment. Then I heard a fluttering of large wings, and, as I looked up on the hill, I saw a huge white seagull come to rest. It stared at me with his wide eyes.

He was a special bird, not only blindingly white, but exceedingly bright eyed as he paced back and forth on the rocks not over 25 feet away. He regarded me for a while, and then flew away. I had passed inspection.

Thoughts crossed my mind: a solitary gull. Out here on a remote island? I had seen no other gulls here. Nor any gulls that white.

Night settled in the tiny harbor, the setting sun splashed its colors across the western sky. The deep pines stood out in bold dark shadows. My boat bobbed in clear waters. I felt at ease and comfortable, as if the wilderness, my boat and I had somehow enjoined in spirit. I thought about being in Albert Leon's favorite place. And my brief visitation with an unusual, white seagull.

On Superior's North Shore, anything was possible. ✵

14

Hard times on Bree's Reef

Discovering a new reef
isn't all it's cracked up to be

I AWAKENED SLOWLY WITH DREAMS that I was in a hammock being rocked back and forth. I opened one eye. The sun was out, shining warmly. In my cove, the water was blue and gentle, a veritable pond of paradise. In its crystalline depths, I could see the bottom beneath my keel. Off to the south, heavily wooded Moss Island seemed still asleep in the early morning.

To the north, a gray cloud hung over the hill overlooking the channel. Rain? Fog? What did it mean?

I did not much care. After more than a week of solo cruising on Lake Superior's northernmost arc, I was in a great mood. I had a deep night's sleep at anchor in a quiet, solitary cove. True to my self-imposed pledge, I stayed away from the radio until I fixed myself a cup of latte and downed a couple of no-aspirin aspirins. Breakfast of champions!

The VHF channel crackled to life to inform me that a small craft warning was being issued. There'd be blustery winds moderate to strong, out of the southwest, 30 gusting to 50 knots. I shook my head, mindful of what a Canadian boater told me: "Up here, move, or you go nowhere. If you listen to them, they'll scare the hell out of you."

I was not unmindful of Murphy's Law, which postulates that anything that can go wrong will. There was even a more specific Murphy's Law for Boaters, which says that anything that can go wrong will—at the worst possible time. Sailors add a corollary: and when you least expect it.

I was having an enjoyable time cruising the northern arc's islands. The worst experiences were behind me. Earlier, I had run into the odd bomb of a storm called "the Green Storm," which turned out to be a rare, progressive derecho with downbursts at over 134 mph in its front wall cloud. I got battered around, but from now on, I was certain, things would only get better. It was the law of averages.

I was having a lot of success anchoring out in these islands using both depth sounders: my electronic one and my mechanical one: the heavy steel centerboard. The latter was infallible, I found, and very accurate. Once we were in too shallow water, the centerboard would bang, vibrate, and let me know to get out of there. It wasn't subtle.

Both were important. Lake Superior's water levels varied from year to year. When I began my voyage in Grand Portage, Minnesota, I had been warned to be careful of rocks because the low was at one of its lowest levels in years. Spring fed, the world's largest freshwater lake had been in decline for years. Later, it would resume higher levels.

I was sailing in the remote and wild archipelago of islands that lay in the northernmost arc of Lake Superior. They extended northeast from Grand Portage, Minnesota, near the United States—Canadian border to about a third of the way across the wild Canadian coastline. Hundreds of Islands. Beautiful, remote and serene—green hillocks rising from the island sea, bearing a spectacular magnificence with high bluffs, bright covers and ancient beaches. These were some of boating's best kept secrets.

Some sailors knew about them but few sailed into them. Local legends had it you could sail up here for days without seeing another boat. That was true. It was a wilderness paradise with its isolated islands, some with their own tiny natural harbors. Now I wanted to sail this area before it got too civilized: the public spotlight was on to make it the world's largest freshwater conservation area, over 10,000 square kilometers in size.

Up anchor! Both Danforths came out of the bottom. I shook them up and down in the water to clean them before I stowed them down in the bilge, where their weight would add to my ballast. Ballast was important to me, since my 20-foot centerboard sloop carried no lead mine keel or ballast bulb down below. The stores' weight was my ballast.

As I made my way down the channel, I keyed my mike to the Thunder

Bay Coast Guard to file my sail plan with them. One hand on the tiller, the other with my mike, I answered their questions.

What was my destination today?

I replied, "CPR Harbor."

Your ETA? I glanced at my chart to estimate my time of arrival when the officer added, "You know.... what time do you want us to come looking for you?"

I chuckled. A little humor there.

Still, his explanation had an ominous ring to it. It was on my mind long after I gave him my ETA. I calculated it generously to get me to CPR Harbor and at anchor with time to spare.

.... ※ ....

The path ahead lay around Moss Island, crossing over Nipigon Straight, and then slipping westward past the tip of Fluor Island, avoiding Dacres Rock. I'd go up a channel of islands: past Puff Island and Mystery Island, to southwest of Agate Island, where I'd head northward. My Canadian chart showed a lot of shallowing and reefs. Lots of reefs.

Getting into CPR Slip would be a little tricky.

In the meantime, I zipped along the inside passage of islands, protected from the lake. High, steep bluffs of pine rose on either side of me. The wind was light so far this morning but growing. The waters were blue, the sun shone down, and I was having a beautiful time, my little boat and me.

A warm glow came over me. It's hard for a big boat sailor to get the exact feeling you have when you're at the helm of a small sailboat.

Persistence is about as small as they come for mighty Superior: Just 20 feet LOA. In this hand-build wood epoxy centerboard sloop, you feel connected to nature. That's because your fanny sits only a dozen inches above the water. Reach over the side with your hand, and you can dabble your fingers in the water's chill 39-degree temperature.

Superior's fresh water is about as good as you'll get anywhere. Some adventurous souls regard it as safe to drink right from the lake. That's water on the northern reaches, away from harbors. Some boaters sail off-shore a couple of miles and then top up their water tanks. Just to be safe, they drop in a purifier tablet or two, as I do. This abundant supply of freshwater is all the more impressive because less than one percent of the world's supply of water is fit to drink. One fourth of the world faces a looming water crisis: they are running out of water. Cities are scrambling. Here I was, aloft in freshwater. All I had to do was scoop it up in my hand.

In growing winds, my little boat swooped over a wave, ducked down behind another, and soared like a thing alive. You are busy. You are never bored. You never think of the office. Not once. Not here on Superior.

I cross north of Mystery Island and gave a wide berth to the rocks of St. Ignance Island's Newash Point. Ahead lay Agate Island.

I shrugged. Despite the rocks, I'd be OK. So far, I'd about done it all on this voyage. I'd just take it easy going in.

To the north and west lay the harbor that a Thunder Bay sailor told me about: CPR Harbor, on St. Ignace Island, also known as Squaw Harbor. This was a special natural harbor, known to few boaters, that nature carved out of an island. As I neared my turn, I found little comfort from my cruising guidebook, which told me about numerous, but unmarked, shoals that the author and others had found over the years. The guidebook warned me to exercise great care in finding my way into the slip.

I throttled my outboard to quarter engine speed. With the wind at our backs and sails furled, *Persistence* didn't slow down a lot as we headed toward the lee shore. We were getting a boost in speed—the wind was coming up. This was not what I wanted.

I stood up in the cockpit seat, snapping on the Autohelm's remote control. This remote was a small handheld device that allowed me to use the Autohelm from most anyplace in the cockpit. I braced myself against the boom, and, with the remote control in one fist, dialed in the course. From my elevated position, I could see ahead and deep into the clear water.

There! That had to be the spit of land that lead to the harbor. I steered toward it. I knew my passage was supposed to be near the shoals and that I had to hug the shore. Off my bow, rocks appeared under the water; I watched my depth sounder rise from 1 foot under the keel to zero feet.

Where was the channel that led me into the harbor?

There was a hollow bump noise, a scraping sound, and I was aground. The tiller twitched in my hand; I was shoved against the boom.

Just like yesterday, when I was trying to make it into Swede Harbor. I'd run aground twice, listening to the steel centerboard rub against the bottom. That was my iron depth sounder at work. I'd throw the outboard into reverse and back off. It worked every time.

I threw the engine into reverse and gave it the gun. *No help.*

This time I was caught. The wind piled us against the rocks; the boat turned sideways, pinioned by the centerboard.

Whump! Whump! Waves and wind began to grind us into the reefs. I was on a lee shore.

I stole a quick glance under the stern. There wasn't enough clearance for the prop. I snicked the gear into neutral, turned off the engine, and hoisted it up on its swing bracket. I didn't want to lose an engine. Not here.

Thunk! Now the rudder was getting a pounding. There was nothing I could do. The wind was catching the mast and careening us to one side.

I ran to the bow with my Danforth and swung the small anchor toward deeper water. I yanked hard, trying to get us off. The anchor popped loose—its flukes would not catch in the rocks. Damn. I tried several more times, but with about the same result. Each time, the anchor would fail to set in the rocks.

Bump! Bam! I did not like the way the boat was caught on the centerboard. The board itself was steel, but it was held into the hull by a single three-quarters inch diameter silicone bronze bolt pinioned through wood. The centerboard was like a long crowbar, exerting tremendous force on the keel. Something could crack, break, or come loose down there. That thought stayed with me.

I yanked on the centerboard pennant. No longer held in place by the steel centerboard, the boat righted itself—and slid further onto the reefs. My friend, the wind, had helped do that.

I stood on the deck, sweltering from my exertions, and wondering what to do next. I looked down into the clear water. Rocks surrounded me; I seemed to be in a pocket of them. The rocky shore was close—maybe 100 feet away.

The wind was increasing as I began pacing the deck, peering down, looking for a way to escape. Shallow water surrounded me. Off in the distance was Agate Island. Somewhere beyond the tall pines, lay CPR harbor.

Rocks surrounded me. I was in a jail of rocks.

.... ❋ ....

I heard a strange noise. Somewhere over that rise, beyond the pines, a noise ripped through the wilderness. It sounded like a chainsaw being started, but in a moment, I could hardly believe my ears. No doubt about it: an outboard engine buzzed its crescendo, and then burbled back to idle.

Where there was an outboard, there was a boat.

I grabbed my mike. "Pan! Pan!" I almost yelled. "I am aground near the entryway to CPR Slip and I need assistance. Particularly from that small boat I just heard starting."

I stuck my head toward the radio speaker. What were the chances that in this wilderness someone had their radio ears on? But in just a few moments, a woman's crisp voice answered. I repeated my plea, adding: "Can I get some help?"

"But of course, you can!" she said.

I sat back down on the deck, mike in hand, somewhat dazed. I still did not know how I would get off this pile of rocks, but I did know help was on its way.

.... ✾ ....

Around the island's tip roared a small aluminum runabout with two large men aboard. They smiled as if relishing a new adventure. At the tiller, one had on a straw panama-type hat, its wide brim shielding his face and his dark sunglasses. Beneath his wide grin, he was dressed in colorful shorts and a T-shirt as if he were on an island in the Caribbean. The other, leaning back on a bow seat, wore shorts and a T-shirt emblazoned with a large red maple leaf on it.

"Eh," the Canadian boaters said, throttling back and staying outside the reefs. "Having a little trouble?"

"Could use some help," I allowed. I wondered what a little fishing boat could do.

"No problem." Gregg Richard was at the tiller. The man in the Canadian T-shirt jumped in the water to his waist and splashed over to my stranded boat.

Ow! I thought that must hurt. I'd been in Superior's chill waters before, but Jake Hayton seemed to take it in stride. In Jake's hand was a heavy line, which I wrapped around my starboard bow cleat.

With Jake in the water shoving my boat, Gregg gave the engine gas: the 35-hp. outboard roared. I could feel my boat's wooden keelson crunch and splinter as they ground against the rock.

We bobbed up and down, alive again. We were in deeper water.

"Thanks" I yelled. I untied the line. Greg circled around with the runabout to pick up Jake. They waved and headed off for the harbor entryway.

I got my centerboard down without difficulty. Much to my relief, nothing was broken.

The grounding damaged the rudder. It flopped back and forth in my hand. I saw why: it had jammed out of its hold-down clip, which was bent out of shape. Without the rudder in its gudgeons, I'd lose control and maybe have the entire rudder come loose and float away.

Grabbing a length of braided line, I looped it over the aft section of the tiller, near the rudder head and made more loops through a teak handhold on the transom. I tightened the hold-down line with some quick half-hitch knots, nothing fancy but fast. I wiggled the rudder back and forth.

It held. The line would hold the rudder in place until I could fix the stainless-steel hold down.

I glanced about. To the north of me, well beyond a point of land, my jaunty Canadian friends were in animated conversation, their boat not moving, engine idling. I motored toward them.

They moved forward again as I approached. Then stopped. I got it: they wanted me to follow them. I began following their movements.

I had discovered all the new rocks I wanted today.

················ ※ ················

I ran eastward under light throttle, mindful of reefs. My Canadian friends were careful to stay close to a spit of L-shaped land, and, looking down, I could see why. There it was, a narrow channel—the very one I was looking for—running east and west. It began close to the shore, dropped off, and, as I followed the channel around a rocky point, headed eastward.

The beauty of CPR harbor opened to me. It was not large, maybe about 500 feet long and about 300 feet at its widest, but it was just right for a few boats. To the west, St. Ignance Island's green hills protected it; to the east and the north, the spit rose in a hillock, covered with pines. At the end of one empty dock, a friendly Canadian boater motioned and helped me come in. I put down fenders, and then threw him my dock lines. I was secure.

Home at last. I felt the sunshine beam down on my face; I looked up at the beautiful blue skies, lined with a few cotton-candy clouds. In this all-weather harbor, I felt only the mildest of breezes—the hills protected us.

A sudden thought crossed my mind: what had happened to *Persistence's* centerboard trunk during the grounding? We had plowed into the rocks at a slow speed but caught on the tip of the centerboard and the rudder. When we came out of the rocks, I heard the crunching underneath.

I pulled up the starboard floorboards. *Water!*

Maybe I had cracked something down there. I ran my flashlight over the joint between the 3/8-inch thick hull and the white oak keelson. There was a puddle of water, but I couldn't feel anything broken. I felt upward with my fingers to the big bronze bolt holding the centerboard in place. No jagged pieces or splinters of wood.

Hauling out my dishwashing pan and my big boat sponge, I went to work to mop up the water. There wasn't a lot down there in *Persistence's* shallow bilge, and when I checked the pan, I guessed I had taken on less than two quarts. I brought out a cloth towel and wiped the bilge area until it was dry.

I waited a bit, watching to see what would happen. I remembered Murphy's Law at Sea. I did not like surprises.

I began to relax, feeling the tension drain out of me. I was lying on the floorboards and starting to sweat. I realized it was not all stress: I still had on my long underwear, polar fleece and wool socks.

Summer had returned! It was warm in beautiful CPR Harbor, and, the Canadians who came out to rescue me had been dressed like they were tourists on a Caribbean cruise. Realizing that I was off the big lake now and thinking I was overdressed, I reached into the centerboard area once again, just to check. Then I'd change if everything was OK.

There was water. We were leaking!

I played my flashlight into the area. Yeah, little beads of water were oozing in from somewhere near the trunk. It was not a lot of water, but this was distressing. Only 3/8ths of lightweight laminated wood separated me from the bottom of the harbor.

Again, I swabbed the area out, both with sponge and towel, and ran my fingers down there to feel that the bilge was dry. I waited. A few minutes later, there was again that seepage, but it seemed to be less. I swabbed, then dried, then felt. The leak seemed to decrease.

Wood! My beautiful little wooden boat was healing itself. The wood was swelling shut, just like wood always does. If I were lucky, it'd take care of the leak.

I stuffed my sponge and towel into the bilges, waited a little more, and hauled them out. The moisture was only a few drops.

I'd come back to check the bilges. In the meantime, I knew I'd still have a boat under me. I just hoped when I returned that the boat would not have the floorboards awash.

.... ✼ ....

I walked down the beach to the *Ogima*, an elderly but sturdy-looking 40-foot steel motor cruiser. Here I met my rescuers, Jake Hayton, who had plunged into the chill water to shove my boat off, and the jaunty skipper of the runabout, Gregg Richard. I also met the large golden lab, Maggie, who served as ship's dog and greeter.

"We talked to the Coast Guard." I recognized the fine Canadian voice of Lynda Blanchette, who had consoled me on the airwaves when I went aground. "They heard your distress call and we told them you were lightly aground and that we were going out to assist you."

"Thank you. I appreciated the help more than you know."

"No problem," she said, smiling. "Cruise Lake Superior and you'll find a few rocks from time to time. Everybody does."

"So, what are you going to name it?" someone asked.

I must have looked puzzled, so they explained: "If you discover a new reef then you have to name it. It's the custom up here."

That night, I went to the logbook the Canadians keep on the island and opened it to a blank page and wrote: "Today we discovered Bree's Reef." I did it with a small smile, not unlike the ones on the faces of my Canadian friends. ✻

15

The last hours of the Edmund Fitzgerald

---⋆⋆⋆---

An ore carrier sinks on Superior

SNOW HAD BEGUN TO FALL, reducing visibility. Waves overran the aft section and shoved their way along the spar deck, putting enormous weight on the hatches. Then they piled up high behind the wheelhouse.

Capt. Ernest McSorley grabbed a handhold to steady himself. The deck tilted; it was difficult to keep a footing on the slippery steel floor. In the pounding of the waves, the wheelsman struggled with the steering: the *Fitz* slewed to starboard and there was no way to keep her on course.

Winds clocked at 80 mph with gusts to 96 mph.; waves piled up 30 feet, with some rogues higher. It was the peak of the storm, and Capt. McSorley's ore boat felt like it was part submarine. It was the worst weather the captain had ever seen.He had already checked down to 14 mph. to ease the boat's laboring hull.

Ahead lay Six Fathom Shoals, extending about five miles north of Caribou Island. The reefs could rip out a ship's bottom.

The *Fitzgerald's* radar was out and the veteran skipper had limited visibility. As the night came on, the lake seemed like a stranger.

About 10 miles behind him, Capt. Bernie Cooper in the oreboat *Arthur M. Anderson* followed the *Fitzgerald's* progress on his radar console.

"He's in close to that Six Fathom spot," Capt. Cooper told the Second Mate. "He's closer than I'd want this ship to be."

"*Arthur M. Anderson*, this is the *Fitzgerald*" A radio message boomed in the wheelhouse for Capt. Cooper. "I have sustained some topside damage; I have some fence rail down, two vents lost or damaged, and I have taken a list. I am checking down. Will you stand by?"

"Roger on that," Capt. Cooper said. "Do you have your pumps going?"

"Both," Capt. McSorley snapped.

Ominous news. The veteran lake captain could decipher what Capt. McSorley was saying:

The thick steel cables encircling the big vessel had snapped. Boarding waves could not have broken them.

The vents' break meant something cataclysmic had happened not on deck but in the below-water ballast tanks. Hydraulic pressure had blasted up from the vessel's bottom and blown off the heavy cast-metal vents.

The pumps each threw 28 tons of water every minute. That meant the *Fitzgerald* had severe leakage down below.

Worse, the 729-foot-long ore carrier carrying 26,116 tons of taconite had suddenly taken a list to starboard.

In the east and entering the lake from Sioux Saint Marie, Duluth pilot Capt. Ced Woodard had just finished an argument with the Swedish captain

"*Pilot*", the ocean-crossing captain snapped, "It's only the lakes."

When the wheelhouse door was ripped off, the Swedish captain turned to Capt. Woodard and gasped. "We've got no business out here."

It was too late. There was no turning back.

The ocean freighter was pounding so hard in the oncoming waves that the pilot thought he would break his kneecaps.

In eight hours, the *Avafors* traveled only 12 miles into the head seas. For two hours, she had not gained a ship's length.

At 5 p.m., winds were gusting to 96 mph. with some wave heights over 30 feet. Capt. Woodard answered a mysterious radio transmission.

"Who in the hell am I talking to?"

"The captain," the strained voice answered.

"It didn't sound like you." Capt. Woodard apologized. He realized he had been talking with his old friend Capt. McSorley. The *Fitzgerald's* captain was under a strain.

⁕

Capt. McSorley could feel the list increasing. Waves routinely overran the Fitzgerald's spar deck and stood 12 feet high. Below him, black water was sloshing about inside the ship. The pumps could not get rid of it fast enough.

He spotted something out of the corner of his eye: Some of the crew had left the aft deckhouse.

Big mistake.

The conditions for the below decks crew were bad and they were trying to get the lifeboats ready. But in these seas, a small open lifeboat would be overpowered and capsize in the huge waves. A small craft could not survive.

"Don't allow anybody on deck," he yelled to his first mate.

They would have to ride it out – there was no other real option. They had to stay with the ship.

As night fell, the *Fitz's* spotlights illuminated a hellish scene. Capt. McSorley made radio contact again: "It's the worst sea I've ever been in."

⁕

At 7 pm, a snow squall hit. *The Anderson's* watch could no longer see the *Fitzgerald*. They still had the big ore carrier on their radar.

They checked on the radio. "We are holding our own," Capt. McSorley said.

A wave train blotted out the *Anderson's* radar. Superior was at her worst.

At 7:25 pm., the *Anderson's* crew squinted into the radar set. Its beams swept the seas ahead of them.

Nothing. The *Fitzgerald* had disappeared. Without even a final distress call, the big ore carrier had disappeared into the depths of Superior

.... ❀ ....

The *Fitzgerald's* sudden death Nov. 10, 1975 is a haunting modern maritime mystery. She's become the *Titanic* of the Great Lakes. The main cause of her sinking is hotly disputed.

Was it faulty hatch covers? A disputed Coast Guard Report argued that the main cause of the *Fitz's* sinking was the collapse of the *Fitz's* heavy steel hatch covers. But other vessels with similar hatch covers had been plying Superior's notorious waters for over 40 years. All had survived.

Perhaps a monster wave had come aboard, piled up behind the wheel-house, and she submarined into the depths. But the *Anderson* had reported such a monster wave and handled it.

Look at Six Fathom Shoals, also reported in the Coast Guard report as a possible main cause of the *Fitz's* sinking. In this scenario, the *Fitz* had cut in too close to the shoal area, bottomed out on a reef, and with its starboard side gouged in, became a sinking ship. Six Fathom Shoals lies about five miles northeast of Caribou Island and is a cluster of reefs with soundings of 8 and 9 fathoms. It is well known to skippers on the northern trek and given a wide berth; charts onboard wheelhouses are marked with a red circle.

It also contains a "new reef" only 5 ¼ fathoms from the surface.

.... ❀ ....

When I was cruising my sailboat on Lake Superior, I carried 27 full-size paper maritime charts. The one covering the Six Fathoms area had a paper "patch" glued over the Six Fathom area, showing a different depth for certain reefs. The new chart update was done after electronic surveying the following spring after the *Fitzgerald's* sinking. It updated the original chart information, which was done in 1917. This turn-of-the-century mea-surement meant the bottom was sounded by dragging a chain behind a boat and measuring the depth when it hit something. If you compared the two chart's depths before and after, there it was: the "new" reef. The *Fitz* had found it.

I had been invited to join a private Canadian group of divers that planned to dive in the Six Fathom area. We wanted to explore the area itself to see what was still down where the *Fitz* had hit bottom. Who knew what we might find? But the impromptu expedition fell apart. I was still in the dark.

One night, I was in Chicago to speak to a yachting group when one mariner pointed to a tugboat out on a point in the harbor. "That's the diver who inspected the reef."

Few people knew about this mysterious diver. Earlier, when I talked with a diving enthusiast from Whitefish Point, I had learned that a diver under private contract had been down on the reef that the *Fitzgerald* had hit. It was not a Canadian operation, even though the reef lay in Canadian waters, but a private diving operation financed by confidential business interests to see what could be found.

The findings might show if the *Fitz* had hit a reef. It might even have evidence of the *Fitzgerald* on the reef. The reef could hold secrets.

"Was that the reef?"

"I really wish I could say," the diver told me on the telephone.

"Well, hypothetically, if a boat like the *Fitz* were to hit a reef, what would you find?" I was pushing it.

"She'd leave more than her calling card."

"Such as?"

He told me that if a 729-foot vessel carrying 26,117 tons of taconite had hit a reef, there would have been something left on the bottom. The impact of the steel upon the rock would leave a gouge in the scum and film that covers most underwater rocks. Bright rock might show. Paint from the bottom of the vessel might have scraped off onto the reef. There might be metal pieces strewn about from where she was holed and where she had scraped her metal plates. Taconite pellets may have spilled from her ruptured hull.

"Is that what you found?

"I really wish I could say."

We left it at that. He had given me several clues to think about. Actually, they were very good clues.

The *Fitz* probably slammed into the new reef in the Six Fathom Shoals. She likely struck near her starboard bottom section, just aft of the pilot house.

The timeline also supported this theory: Before she went into the Shoals area, she was in radio contact with the following *Anderson* and reported no problems. It was only minutes after she emerged from the other side of the shoals that Capt. McSorley broadcast his ominous message of fence cable down, ballast vents broken, pumps on, and a list.

.... ❁ ....

A rogue wave 45 feet high shoved its way aboard her lowed spar deck and roared along until it piled high behind the pilothouse. The added weight made the bow dig in; this time, it was not coming back up. Dark waters rushed up, shattering the ordinary window-pane glass of the wheelhouse. Onrushing waters slammed into the wheelsman, the first mate and the captain and carried them to the aft section of the small cabin.

The *Fitz* submarined, bow-first down into the depths at about 28–30 mph. It hit the bottom 530 feet below, plowing a path in the mud. The 253-foot aft section twisted off and turned upside down, its crew trapped inside.

The bow section remained upright, as if it were ready to sail on. The wheelhouse door on the port side was open and its latch locked in the open position. The heavy steel door would have been closed and locked tight during the storm.

A short distance away from the hull, lying face down in the bottom mud, lies the body of a man. He was a crewmember who had survived the nightmare ride to the bottom.

Once the hull had come to rest, by the flickering illumination of the emergency lights, he had forced open the wheelhouse door and locked it in open position. With his last burst of strength, he swam out of the pilothouse. But at 500 feet below the surface, his personal flotation device had collapsed; it had no buoyancy.

It was an incredible feat of bravery but a doomed survival attempt. He sank back down into the mud and rests forever beside his ship.

.... ❁ ....

A few years back, I sailed a catamaran along the Shipwreck Coast leading to Whitefish Point. I glanced to my northwest and I realized that only about 15 miles out the *Fitzgerald* remains forever beneath the waves.

They could have been at the Point in about an hour. The *Big Fitz* had been so close to safety. So close and yet so very far. ❁

16

The legacy of the old fishing guide

---☆☆☆---

A dream of wilderness that came true

IT WAS A WONDERFUL DAY for cruising solo, with bright skies, waves less than a meter in height, and light winds out of the southwest. I was returning after my overnight stay in the Slate Islands. A problem came up as I neared the Government Dock at Rossport, Ontario, the tiny fishing hamlet on the Big Lake's northernmost arc. There was no room for my 20-foot centerboard sloop.

Circling alongside the dock, I saw the dock boy come out of his shack, curious. "Where can I tie up?" I hollered across the water.

"Next door. Lady says it's OK."

Odd, I thought. Someone would loan me his personal dock space? Back in the Twin Cities, I boated in waters where private docks were jealously guarded. No sailboats welcome

Past the Government Dock, I saw a private dock extending out into the water. As I headed toward it, a woman looked up and began walking out toward me.

I signaled my request to dock and she waved back. *Hospitable*. But things were going too well.

Wham. I heard the unmistakable sound of my steel centerboard banging against the bottom; I felt the familiar vibration in the hull. About 30 feet from the dock, we ground to a halt.

We had done it again. Run aground on a rock.

We were old hands at this on Superior. "Just a moment," I said, ducking below and yanking on the centerboard pennant. With the centerboard up, we scooted over the rocks and alongside the dock.

"Thanks, " I said. "I appreciate it."

"You're welcome," Colleen Kenney said, taking my dock lines and helping me tie up. "We have the space, and you are welcome to use it."

.... ❀ ....

I was on a month-long voyage single-handing my home-built 20-foot centerboard sloop, *Persistence*, through the archipelago of islands in the northern arc of Lake Superior. In this marine wilderness, verdant islands rose majestically from clear blue waters, and, wonder of wonders, I found tiny island harbors into which I could wriggle my boat to anchor for the night. I wanted to voyage through this island archipelago while it was still an ancient, natural world, not yet touched by civilization—and there was some talk of making it into some kind of marine conservation area.

Where I sailed, time had seemed to stand still. Beauty was everywhere. The islands had not changed from the days when the ancient voyageurs paddled through from New France in their birchbark canoes. Freshwater in transparent clarity remained.

.... ❀ ....

As I tied P*ersistence* up to the private dock, Colleen Kenney came over: "You should meet my father." I was a guest at the waterfront home of Capt. Ray Kenney, a grand old man of the lake and a legend. I figured I'd say hello.

I paused to admire a battered old steel-hulled powerboat up on blocks. With her plumb bow, the *Yennek* once must have been a powerful looking brute punching through Superior's waves. Her dented hull was covered with metal patches and her wooden cabin showed rot. I moved my hand along her hull. Her once bright silver-painted hull was scratched and dented; rust showed through. The entire hull near the waterline had a series of creases, bumps, and hollows, the result of decades of warfare. She was old and worn, but to my eyes she was still a noble vessel. I wondered how she came to be rusting away at the water's edge.

At the house, a soft-spoken white-haired old man greeted me as he looked up from his wheelchair. He was Capt. Ray Kenney, a former school principal who had taught in Canadian schools for 40 years during the winters but "boated summers."

His picture window overlooked the beautiful Rossport harbor and his old boat up on blocks. The *Yennek*, I learned, is his name spelled backwards. It all started to fit together.

"Some say throw it in the garbage," Ray said. "But it is almost a historic boat."

At age 91, the old skipper's eyes still twinkled blue and he told me he was glad to see me cruising the lake, as he had done for so many years.

He asked me if I had been to The Slate Islands and I told him I had overnighted there, all alone at Lampton Cove, near an old mine.

"See any caribou?"

"A big one with a rack of antlers and huge hooves," I said. "Just browsing his evening meal."

The Slates were the southernmost home of this Arctic animal. The old fishing guide smiled. He'd been there many times. As I sat beside him, sipping coffee, the man in the wheelchair spun tales of his *Yennek* about how he had taken scientists, adventurers, journalists and cameramen offshore to the Slates.

He and the *Yennek* helped the Cousteau series explore this part of Lake Superior. *National Geographic* magazine chartered her for a feature article and photography on the Slate Islands.

"A cameraman wanted to get a scene out in the rough seas," Ray recalled. "So, we took the *Yennek* out into some big waves. In the troughs we were so far down we were out of sight."

"Get the pictures?"

"When we saw it later, the film just showed the flag above the waves. He never got any pictures of the heavy stuff." The cameraman who was gung-ho to get out to film Superior's vaunted storm waves had frozen up behind his camera.

Ray had met Superior's famed "Three Sisters," a combination of three waves, each larger than the first. "You get on top of the Three Sisters on a boat like the *Yennek*, you get quite a ride. But be careful or you can bury yourself."

He added: "If you make a mistake out there on Superior you

usually pay for it."

Ray's *Yennek*, a 28-footer, was built in 1947 with an all-steel bottom "thick and tough," Ray said. "Armor plate." She was originally powered by a big inboard Lycoming engine, which was replaced by a Chrysler T120 in 1948.

"You get storms with 45-foot waves off Battle Island," he recalled. On this island were diesel tanks anchored with steel straps 42 feet above the water level. "We had a storm come in and toss them in the bush." He added, "A 500-gallon tank anchored at the base of the lighthouse disappeared. They never found it again."

He also had memories of the *Edmund Fitzgerald*. The "Big Fitz," he said, "we saw from about a half mile away. Boy, was she a rusty-looking old hulk." He recalls saying to his wife, "Does she ever look in tough shape."

Capt. Kenney was "just going to work" the day of the *Fitzgerald's* terrible storm but when he exited the Schreiber Channel and powered into Superior's open seas, he hit "tremendously big waves." It was a northeaster late in the season on November 10. Capt. Kenney had to get some campers off an island, no matter how rough the weather was. They were really glad to see him, but on the return trip, the campers became terrified. Waves worked their way over the deck and the mighty *Yennek* lumbered and pitched.

"Don't worry'"" one man vowed: "We'll NEVER come back."

On that day, Capt. Kenney recalled: "The waves hit you, and hit you so hard, it was like someone taking a big, big sledgehammer and hitting you."

The *Yennek* made it back to Rossport to drop off its shaken and unhurt passengers, but that night the *Fitzgerald* went down with a loss of all hands. "When you try to compete with nature, man's best works are pretty fragile." Capt. Kenney reflected. And as for Superior, he told me: "Love it, respect it, particularly, its might."

And as for the camper who promised that if he ever made it back from the lake, he'd never come back—he kept his word. "Never saw him again."

The grand old man had many passions for the wilderness and the freshwater he had plied for so many years. He told me of his dreams of a marine conservation area that he supported vigorously. With his voyages, he had done a lot to make people aware of this special wilderness up north.

.... ❋ ....

I sat up on my bunk and knew something was wrong. There was a heaviness that hung in the air. Peering out *Persistence's* forward hatch, I saw dark clouds heading our way.

I snapped on my VHF weather radio. "Strong thunderstorm warning," the Canadian weather service announced, "with high winds."

I saw that an elderly couple, Harold and Joyce Dahlgren, of West Point, Iowa, had their boat tied up on Ray's dock. They were getting ready to go out in their 17-foot runabout.

Concerned, I walked over to see if they'd heard the storm warning.

"We're not going far," Joyce said. "Just into the islands. Ray is coming with us."

"Where are you going?"

"Wherever Ray wants to go."

I learned that when the Iowa couple came to Canada about 27 years ago, they fell in love with the little village of Rossport and the nearby islands. "We met Ray and we used to go out with him in his *Yennek* until it got too old to go," Joyce said. "He's still showing us some of his favorite spots."

"He used to take us out," Joyce explained. "Now we take him out."

Some motion on the dock caught my eye. I turned and stared.

"Look there," I said. I stepped forward, ready to help.

Ray was down on his hands and knees, crawling down the dock. Worried, I asked, "Does he need help?"

"Naw," Harold drawled. "He prefers to do it himself."

I looked closer. Capt. Kenney's wheelchair was near the water's edge and the old fishing guide was on the dock on all fours with some obvious pride.

"Need help?" Harold casually asked the crawling man.

Ray shook his head. No.

"He really prefers to do it himself," the Iowa boater repeated, mostly for my benefit.

Capt. Kenney crawled into the boat, settled himself and Harold started the engine. I watched as the small runabout cut a wake through the blue waters out toward Quarry Island. Soon angry clouds swept in; thunder rumbled, and the day grew dark. I saw lightning flashes over the islands. I ran to my sailboat and ducked into the cabin before the rain came sheeting down.

I thought of the old captain and the Iowa couple out in their little fishing boat.

Rain turned to hailstones. I could hear them thump and pound on my wooden cabin roof. I was secure and dry—but what about them? Should I go out after them? And where, exactly, had they gone?

After a while, the storm blustered off, the sun came out again, but I still saw no sign of the old mariner and his party.

Then, from somewhere in the islands and through the setting sun's rays, came the sound of an outboard's high-powered whine. Their boat cut a shining wake in the harbor.

I hurried over to their dock. "Any trouble with the squall?"

"Oh," the Iowa man said, "we saw the storm coming, so we just ducked into a little cove and waited it out. No problem. Then we went back to fishing."

"Catch anything?"

"Only a couple little ones."

Obviously, they had been to one of Ray's secret fishing spots and had done well. I glanced in the boat and looked at Ray.

Beneath the brim of his long-billed fishing cap, the old man's eyes twinkled proudly.

.... ✸ ....

Years later, I got the dreaded telephone call. "Ray has passed away," Joyce Dahlgren told me. "I thought you'd like to know." Indeed, I did. My memory flashed back to when Capt. Ray Kenney, age 91, crawled down the dock by himself and then, with his Iowa friends, headed out onto his beloved Superior.

Ray lies buried in the Rossport cemetery, near a small church, in a quiet meadow with a sweeping view of the Rossport harbor. Long ago, Ray had arrived in this tiny Ontario village with his bride to make a home for himself, at first for summers, and later, for the rest of his life. It was a good resting place for the old guide.

His beloved *Yennek*? There was nothing to be done. The boat had become a rusting hulk They had to cut her up and haul the salvage away for scrap metal.

But they saved small mementoes that they sank in the waters off the islands he had loved. Her steering gear lies in the deep waters off Simpson Island, where Ray and the *Yennek* sailed so often. Some of her instruments went to the Iowa couple, because they were part of family.

His daughter, Colleen Kenney, carries on for him. He taught her some of his old fishing holes, and now she takes people out for tours of the islands and fishing, just the way the old fishing guide did.

But a part of his legacy was yet to come. He told me many times of his interest and his work to save a large portion of Lake Superior. His interest was the northern area I had just sailed through. The Big Lake was changing through his lifetime and he wanted the northern shores to remain an unspoiled wilderness. It was an ambitious undertaking: the proposed Lake Superior National Marine Conservation Area of Canada would save about 10,000 square kilometers and encompass one-seventh of Superior. It would be the world's largest freshwater conservation area. ✺

17

The Mac comes back

───────────────✩✩✩───────────────

An old-time design hath its charms

HER PATH LAY UP THE FAIRWAY, past another dock, and around a large steel schooner. Not only was that tricky maneuvering under sail, but it was an upwind slog all the way. As I watched, the small, wooden boat named the *Paul La Plante* nimbly scooted between two other boats and, with a small thump, came to a stop on the wooden dock in front of me. No harm came to her wooden stem or to the boat—and I could see why.

"The bobstay makes a good brake," joked the skipper.

You don't see many bobstays on boats these days. On the other hand, you don't see many boats like the one he was sailing.

His make-do "brake" was the stout line that led from the bowsprit to the stem. It had taken the light impact of the boat's bump into the dock. The wooden bow was unmarred.

I recognized her as a Mackinaw boat, a design from about 1780—the working days of sail on Superior. There was a lot of seagoing heritage built into this old-fashioned wind ship. The tiny two-masted replica gave the impression she could handle big waters.

The boat also was a look into our maritime past.

Superior hadn't changed. But boats sure had.

.... 🎊 ....

"Hop in." David Cooper handed me a PFD, which was one of the few touches of modernity I could see on the Mac. I began to board amidships, but the park ranger shook his head. "You've got the helm."

Cooper picked up a long oar and with a shove, we got underway. Our path lay behind the North House's schooner *Hjordis*. The wind was whipping us toward it, but with Cooper working the oar, we maneuvered around the schooner's aft section. Minutes later, we were out of the fairway and running downwind under bare poles.

Cooper raised the jib. I noticed how light the tiller pressure was, and, looking behind me, I saw how the water parted off the sharp stern, like the water from a duck's behind. There was no gurgling noise or immersed transom to slow the boat.

Looking into the bilge, I saw water slopping about—rainwater. Cooper confirmed that the construction was "pretty tight." He said, "it does the usual spring swelling and soak-up after the launch for a few days, but then you can go a week or two the rest of the season without having to pump." He added, "Barring heavy rains."

We were past the docks and into the historic Grand Marais harbor. First, Cooper raised the forward sail on its gaff rig, then the large sail in front of me. Both went up easily, but I found that I shared space with the foot of the sail: When we tacked, I'd have to duck under the boom.

We picked up speed.

I got an impression that this was a lot of mast, rigging and sails for an 18-foot boat. The ketch rig had the obvious advantage of spreading its 242 square feet of sail in three sails: In heavy weather, the boat could balance off on jib and mizzen, rather than sailing on jib, mizzen and main, or, by just reefing the main. But the rigging took up cockpit space, until the sails went up. Then we still had a lot of lines in the cockpit to fiddle with.

"The gaff-rigged ketch is not easy to singlehand," Cooper confirmed. "You end up with a handful of lines. Housekeeping—keeping them coiled down, neat and organized—is important."

The boat had a good feel to it. "She carries a lot of canvas for her size with plenty of get up and go in good winds," Cooper said. He recalled that one North House boat builder called her "a little Ferrari."

Cooper added, "She even ghosts along well in very light airs, when most boats would be stalled out."

.... ✿ ....

We ran downwind through the Grand Marais harbor, hooked a turn to port and began a deep reach toward the lighthouse at the harbor entryway. Beyond lay a heavy fog bank on Superior, blown in by the winds.

The boat seemed a little tender, I thought, by the way Cooper used his weight. When he was on the windward side of the cockpit, the boat stayed upright, but when he moved to leeward, the boat followed him almost down to the gunwales. Cooper quickly corrected. He was good ballast.

Cooper told me that these boats used to carry 600 pounds of ballast (usually stones) or cargo. Stone ballast is practical since you toss it overboard as you take on cargo. We had 400 pounds of moveable lead ballast onboard and we also could count on moveable ballast in the form of Cooper, a big guy at over 220 pounds. That would suffice, provided he kept his weight to windward. I observed he seemed inclined to make the right moves. Superior's waters are cold. Cooper did not want to get wet.

I had to duck under the mizzen's swinging low boom, which came up to about my shoulder level, or else it would hit my head. The boom could not be raised: there was lot of sail and only so much mast up there. The answer for me was to crouch down when the tiller went over. Since I was in charge of the tiller, that wouldn't be a real problem. I'd know when to duck.

"That way." Cooper waved his arm toward the harbor entryway. We were going out onto the open waters.

As we came off our reach and into a broad run, the Mac seemed to come alive. We had a lot of sail up on a tiny boat and the thought came to me: "No wonder they liked these boats so much in the old days: they were small craft hot rods."

They had to be quick. As a commercial fishing boat, with one or two North Shore fisherman aboard, a craft had to be speedy to get its catch back to shore in time for the fresh fish to be cleaned and preserved in a salty brine.

The tiller was steady in my hands and the sails felt balanced. I began to relax until I saw what lay ahead.

"Fog out there," I said.

We charged into heavy fog banks. The wind was gusty, perhaps up to

25 mph. That was a lot for a little boat with all sails up and drawing hard.

I peered ahead, but I couldn't see very far. There was a golden luminescence in the fog bank as the sun shone down on us; the waters seemed a beautiful greenish-yellow in the glow.

"We just lost the lighthouses," I said.

"I can still see the top of that one." Cooper wasn't bothered.

.... ❋ ....

I settled down and started to relax. Two things let me do that: first, I knew that I had a built-in compass, even if the boat did not have one. We were reaching into the wind. All I had to do was to come about and follow a reciprocal course to the wind. Fog or no fog, that would get me in close enough to the lighthouses to find our way to the breakwater.

And second, I saw that Cooper had tucked a small hand-held VHF in a black waterproof bag under the bow area. There was a Coast Guard Station in Grand Marais and if we got into tough shape, such as losing our way in the fog or even capsizing in the waves, Cooper could call and get help. Later, Cooper told me he also had a small GPS tucked away in the black bag.

In the heavy fog, the waves came in yellow-green lumps that the little boat rode over like a duck. The sails held their pressure; the hull glided forward, as if it were running on rails. I remembered: we had a long keel from stem to stern.

"She points good," I said.

"Yeah, and we don't even have the centerboard down," Cooper said. He was enjoying himself.

I felt like we could glide forever in the golden fog. My only concern was that Grand Marais was the only port for many miles on this rock-ribbed north shore, and that there might be some incoming traffic. We couldn't see anything beyond 75 feet. But then again, I didn't think anyone would be dumb enough to be out in pea-soup fog.

A thought came to me. I kept my mouth shut.

Cooper gave the signal. I turned the boat into the wind, and we came about on a reciprocal course back to the entryway. Here again, the Mac surprised me: we bounded around without fuss; we didn't heel much, either. This little boat—with no reefs in its sails, without its full complement of ballast and without its centerboard down—handled well on Superior.

.... ❈ ....

Back inside the harbor, we headed toward our dock space—the one we had some difficulty getting out of. Now we'd have to sail upwind.

Cooper called the shots from his position at the front of the cockpit. I peered ahead: the fairway did not look all too wide to maneuver in, with several docks extending out into it. Along each side of the docks were boats of all descriptions and at the end of the one we wanted was the big schooner, Hjordis.

"Head straight for the docks," Cooper instructed. "Then when I give the signal, tack to port." We seemed to hang onto our tack for a long time and when we were within maybe 20 feet of the dock, Cooper yelled, "tack."

He grabbed the small jib by hand. Instead of using a jib sheet, he wrestled the jib in the direction he wanted. Wind pressure swung the bow smartly around.

We headed toward the awaiting rocks. We came close, then tacked again.

Cooper had timed it right. Our zigzag had brought us into position for the final zag into the dock space behind the schooner and between two other fragile looking wooden boats.

We glided into the dock and I straightened the little boat out. I noticed we had come in with a little bump.

Cooper's emergency brake—the line on the bowsprit—had worked just fine again.

.... ❈ ....

Cooper and I later talked about our ride. "We don't hesitate to take her out in reasonable seas and winds," he said. "We've had her out in 5 to 6-foot seas, which are enough for an 18-footer, and she rides them like a duck, stays reasonable dry and in these seas the cockpit coamings do an amazing job of keeping most of the green water out."

"Ten to 20-knot winds and 1 to 3- foot seas are the most comfortable for us laid-back small-craft sailors," He said. "But as always, the boat can handle a lot more than the crew."

This was my first ride in a such a historic design. After I got used to the gaff rig, it seemed to be a model of simplicity with its mast rings and laced-on sails. Even in today's winds, we did not reef the 242-square feet of sail and it didn't seem like we needed to. The Mac handled wind gusts well, since the gaff-rigged sail area is located lower to the hull than a contemporary Bermuda-rigged boat. We sailed her without her full 600 pounds of internal ballast, yet she hadn't been tender. The Mac had a good angle tacking into the wind, though her centerboard was not down. She had a good turn of speed. In fact, I thought she was downright speedy.

"Some sailors have a little trouble adapting to the balance of the ketch and the feel of the gaff rig," Cooper pointed out. He said that his gaff-rig mentor, North House volunteer Dennis Bradley, had coached him on the *Paul La Plante's* idiosyncrasies, such as the art of manhandling the jib to help with tacking. This is what he had done to give us control coming into our berth earlier.

"The gaffs have a mind of their own and it takes a firm hand on the sheets to control them in a jibe." He recalled that one student had the sheet jerk out of his hand during a jibe, causing the mizzen gaff to get a serious swing going. "This resulted in a 360-degree turn around the mast and a huge wadded up mess of a mizzen sail hanging from the upper mast," he said. "On a small boat, after the initial excitement, it was easy to sort this mess out." But he added, "On a bigger vessel, it could have been dangerous."

The *Paul La Plante* was a fine little boat. It delighted me to take the helm of this centuries-old design and learn more about the boats of our mariner forefathers. It inspired me. They were, I reminded myself once again, very clever and knowledgeable people and we could learn something from them.

The sea had not changed. ❀

18

Midnight crossing

★★★

*Where was the light
this dark and stormy night?*

OUR SHIPBOARD BAROMETER HAD BEEN DROPPING—an ominous sign that the storm was coming close. The weather channel had issued small craft warnings. Earlier, we considered getting off the lake and staying overnight at Ontonagon Harbor, but our navigator nixed this: "If the storm arrives as expected from the north to northeast quadrant, we'll be pinned on the south shore for days by 10-foot waves."

The catamaran's twin 27-horsepower diesels purred at 2,800 rpm. I checked my knotmeter and then the Global Positioning System: the cat was moving at 6.8 knots. Good enough: Our calculations called for us to be inside the breakwaters of the Keweenaw Waterway before the storm was scheduled to arrive. The forecast called for it to hit sometime early in the morning, at about 1:30 a.m. or so. We'd arrive at the breakwaters and gain the protection of the inland waterway at about 12:30—and we'd be secure at harbor about halfway up the waterway by 4 a.m.

It would be an all-night run for us on Lake Superior.

The race against the storm, now in deadly earnest, was on.

Night enveloped us. Alone at the helm of the 35-foot catamaran, *Tullamore Dew*, I looked about: it seemed as if the world ended with the boat. Below, the water moved darkly, but I had lost my sense of direction and motion. At the bow, a white running light gleamed into the fog, but I could see little further than that in the dark. We were running blind on this dark sea; I hoped we did not come across another boat, or find some object floating in the water. I watched the digital readout on the compass rise, then kicked the rudder to port to correct several degrees. The big cat came back to course, the twin rudders biting deep in the chill waters.

I was alone in a world of fog and darkness. Somewhere ahead lay the Keweenaw Waterway, our exit off the lake. The waterway cuts through the Keweenaw Peninsula, a unique finger of rocky land that juts far into Superior. It is famous for its lake effect, which makes it one of the snowiest places in the Nation. "This place was made to catch snow," a resident once told me. In the winter, it can draw up to 32 feet of snow; inhabitants carve tunnels in the snowbanks to get to their homes. In the summer, it catches a wild assortment of storms. I hoped we'd be off the lake before a storm descended.

Despite our charts and GPS, we had to be careful finding the western entry This fog-shrouded night, if I approached the stone entryway one or two degrees off course, I'd run up on a rocky shore. Or hit a stone entry wall. I knew that inside the cabin, the skipper, Joe Boland, and navigator, Thom Burns, and crewmember, Bruce Boland, were following my progress on their navigation gear. At least I hoped they were.

I heard raucous laughter. Stealing a glance through the companionway hatch, I saw that they huddled over the main cabin table—playing cards. Apparently, they didn't share my concerns. I wondered who was winning.

I turned to face the direction that the storm might come from. I could almost feel the chill of the low approaching us. I huddled inside my foul-weather gear; my glasses misted up. I had both gloved hands on the destroyer-type steering wheel. I got some protection from the canvas dodger that covered the forward section of the cockpit, but that also presented a problem for me. At well over six feet in height, Joe Boland could look over the dodger, but I could only peer over its top edges. I solved that problem by standing on a sturdy ice chest we kept in the cockpit. Then I could stand high enough to see something in the onrushing dark.

I read the compass and checked it with the GPS. I was holding the boat on course for the fog-shrouded Keweenaw entryway, now only hours away.

"We'll make it OK," I thought to myself.

.... ❊ ....

A low, moaning sound came closer and closer. I peered into the darkness, but I could see nothing. With a shriek, it descended; I could feel the sailboat caught in a great rushing of wind. *Tullamore Dew* threw her bows to one side, then began a slide to port, her deck canting as if one bow was on an elevator heading down. I spun the wheel hard to starboard, but there was no stopping her.

I lost control.

With a gut-lurching crash, the port bow plunged into a wave trough. I spun the wheel—she lurched upward for a moment, then righted herself.

"What was that?" Shouts came from the cabin. The storm had interrupted their card game.

"I couldn't hold her when that first gust came through."

It was a short-lived example of the ferocity of Superior's weather. A microburst from the approaching front threw the big cat about as if it were a toy.

"But she seems steady now," I said.

.... ❊ ....

I glanced at my watch. We had received our first knock at about 11 p.m. We'd had a foretaste; when the real storm arrived, it would be a major blow.

The waves had grown. It wasn't the size of the waves that made my heart pound, it was the speed with which they roared. A wave train would hit one bow, causing a shudder, then the wave would pass underneath, dipping the bow, only to repeat the whole motion across the second bow.

We pounded along, up, down, and sideways, as if on a watery elevator without a sense of direction.

.... ❊ ....

We sped toward the entryway somewhere ahead in the dark. The entryway itself had claimed many shipwrecks. I glanced below and saw that Thom, the navigator, now was concentrating on his charts and his GPS navigation equipment. The card game was over.

We'd have to get in close to see the entryway's massive stone piers.

The skipper, Joe, took over the helm, and I moved forward in the cockpit.

Somewhere, the north breakwall extended far out into Superior. At its end, a lighthouse flashed a white light. We should be able to see it on a clear night for miles at sea. It also had a foghorn sounding. On the south breakwall, there should be another light.

"Well, we're here," Thom announced.

"But where?" Joe wanted to know. And so did I.

"The GPS says we're just off the pier. It's right ahead of us."

I could see only fog and blackness. If we went in too close, we might end up on shore or smash up against a breakwater.

Minutes passed. The skipper began a slow circle.

I saw something off the starboard bow. Odd, I thought; my first impression was that it was nothing, but as I waited a few seconds, there it was again: something bloomed in the fog bank.

"Over there." I yelled to Joe, pointing. "A light."

"That's it!" The cat lurched forward in the swells.

Out of the fog loomed a black stone pier.

"But which one?" Joe asked. If the pier ahead of us was the south one, we'd end up on the rocky shore. Only the north pier would give us safe entry to the canal.

"North pier," I said.

"South pier," someone else guessed. Damn.

"North—south—which one?" Joe throttled the diesels back and began creeping forward. We'd take our time and not go in too close, too fast.

The fog lifted for a moment. It was the north pier.

To starboard was the south breakwater, but it had no light on it I could see. Nor was there a foghorn.

Joe lined up *Tullamore Dew* for the entrance, edging the diesels up a notch.

Inside the piers, the walls grew around us. But it was not at all what we expected. The waterway was pitch black and filled with fog. There were no lights. The air felt like the inside of a tomb. The narrowness surprised me; I felt as if I could lean out with one hand and touch a wooded bank.

Below us, we had shallow waters. This would be tricky.

Joe had the big cat edging ahead at fast idle.

A crewmember grabbed a flashlight and made his way to the bow pulpit. He shone the beam ahead and to the sides.

I saw a light. A navigation signal of some sort, I presumed. I pointed, and we began steering toward it.

"Wait!" The crewmember frantically waved his arms. "It's a yard light. From a farm."

Joe veered the cat off, and we were back in the channel, marked by buoys.

Our new strategy was to steer from buoy to buoy. Our problem was that we could not see the buoys in the fog until we practically ran into them.

Thom entered the GPS waypoints for the twenty-three buoys. Joe proceeded at 1.5 to 2.0 knots, using the cat's depth meter to stay in the middle of the channel. Bruce and I kept watch with flashlights to find buoys and day markers.

We motored through the night until we saw the first pink flushes on the horizon: morning was coming. Ahead lay the lift bridge that linked the twin cities of Hancock and Houghton, Michigan. Thom called ahead on the VHF radio; the bridge captain answered, asking our clearance height.

"Fifty feet," Thom replied into the mike.

"Come ahead." We idled forward, waiting for the bridge to open. Then the rumble of the largest lift bridge in the world filled our ears. To the north, on the Houghton side, was the Portage Lake Marina, just a short way past the vertical lift bridge. I looked ahead, and sighed: Yes, there was a slip open. We brought the cat in to rest.

I glanced at my watch: it was 4:30 a.m.

The long night had ended. We were off Superior.

.... ❈ ....

I sat back in the cockpit, feeling the wind on my back. The morning was brightening around me, making last night's adventures seem remote. It came home to me we had tiptoed along a narrow line with potential disaster looming at us.

We also got lucky. ❈

19

The longest night

---⭐⭐⭐---

At an old silver mine—a strange storm

THE WOODEN DOCK WAS OLD AND ROUGH. I found a place to tie up my boat about halfway down the east side. After I had put out my fenders, I had a close look at the ancient timbers. Decades of ice and water had scoured them raw. Where the wood had worn away, metal spikes stuck out like knives.

Not the best place to dock a little wooden boat

Night was approaching as I trudged down the dock toward land. I found some rough lumber behind the old General Store. Sorting through the pile, I found an ancient plank four inches thick, a foot deep, and ten feet long. It was heavy. I grunted as I hefted it atop my shoulder.

At the boat, I tied a line around each end of the plank and lowered it down the pilings to the level of my boat's wooden rub rail. This "camel" would hold my boat away from the metal spikes on the pilings. I lowered white rubber fenders between the boat rub rail and the camel.

Provided that the camel didn't slip between the pilings or the fenders didn't get pushed aside, my boat would be secure in Silver Islet.

.... ✺ ....

Just a few klicks away, out on Superior, lay a small, historic island. I could see it from my cockpit. In July 1868, a survey party rowed out to inspect this unimpressive hunk of rock 90 feet across, 8 feet at its highest, and polished smooth by the storm waves that overran it.

The Montreal Mining Company owned this North Shore wilderness, but the Canadian government was about to levy a two-cents-an-acre tax. The surveyor's job was to figure out which of the several thousands of acres around Thunder Cape were worth keeping. The Montreal Mining company was thrifty; they didn't want to pay the two-cent tax.

On the island, one man saw something shiny. In the shallow water lay a startling white line. Twenty feet at its widest, the brightness ran from the rock into the lake.

He splashed into the water and pried out a lump of rock. It was pure silver.

.... ※ ....

His enthusiasm was short lived. The survey party discovered that the silver lay below water. They could only mine the ore through the small island.

They soon learned that storms could wash over the island, tear away protective cribs and even roll away solid rock. After repeated failures, the mining company gave up. They sold the mine for $225,000 to American industrialist Alexander Sibley.

Sibley hired the boldest mining engineer he could find, Capt. William Belle Frue, who arrived by boat in 1870. Frue built a rock pile six feet high on the island and climbed to the top to study the lake's action. When a violent storm rose from the southeast, he watched the waves build and march toward his tiny rock pile. He was stranded.

It was only after the storm had blown itself out that a rowboat could come from shore to rescue the wet and freezing engineer.

Impressed, Frue built a virtual fortress around the island. Twenty thousand square feet of heavy timber became a six-foot-high breakwall, held by iron shafts two inches thick.

Another storm slammed into the fortress; waves overran the breakwall. That night from the mainland, Frue peered into the darkness of his besieged fortress.

When the storm subsided, Frue rowed out to see that Superior had demolished 200 feet of breakwater, torn open a coffer dam, and filled the mine shaft. The two-inch thick iron rods were so bent that a miner half-joked: "They might as well have been my wife's hairpins."

Frue rebuilt the tiny island again, this time encircling it with a crib of timber filled with rock to break the waves. Men worked 18-hour days to make it rise 18 feet above the lake, with a base that extended 75 feet.

It expanded the island to ten times the size of the original rock. On the cribwork and island were the shaft house, four large boardinghouses, machine shops, blacksmith and carpenter shops, a boiler room, offices and clubrooms, a lighthouse, a system of range lights, storehouses, and buildings filled with mining machinery, huge engines, and massive docks. At its peak, 480 men worked there.

.... ▩ ....

Silver Island boomed. Between 1872 and 1874, the miners took out a million ounces of silver ore. The stock of the company rose from $50 a share to $25,000. Speculators made a fortune on the stock.

As the mine went deeper, the shaft cut through fissures; water began to pour in. Miners shored up the cracks as best they could and brought in heavier water pumps. The battle against Superior had begun.

Storms slamming in from the southeast were the deadliest. One December gale battered the fortress hard enough to carry away 350 feet of cribbing, 20,000 feet of lumber, and tons of huge boulders. Superior picked up huge rocks and tossed them about like hailstones.

In the mine, miners worked cold and wet. They descended in a cage deep below Superior's surface. Their only light was the flickering illumination of their head candles. Walls dripped with moisture. They worked in constant danger of flooding. They got paid $68 a month, but the company docked them $14 for room and board.

In two years, the shoreline boasted a church (complete with widow's walk around its steeple), schoolhouse, post office, and housing for five hundred people. They built a General Store. The directors brought in their own yacht, the *Silver Spray*.

Below the surface, the mine reached a depth of 1,230 feet. Fifteen levels intersected the main shaft. The lode became elusive, sometimes narrowing, then widening. Huge pumps ran continuously.

In 1884, the mine ended. One story is that the islet's supply of coal for the pumps lay on board a steamer, immobilized across the Big Lake at Houghton, Michigan. Its drunken captain had allowed the vessel to become frozen in. On the islet, miners fed their boilers every piece of wood they could bring over from the mainland, but by March, the lake gained. Fires went out and pumps stopped. The tunnels flooded and Lake Superior claimed its own.

Another, less romantic version of the tale, is that the mine became unprofitable. Miners had to go deeper and farther for less ore, at greater expense and danger. In 1884, when the price of silver dropped, the mine became too expensive to operate.

The world's richest underwater silver mine was dead.

.... ❈ ....

From my sailboat, I took out my binoculars and scanned the big hunk of rock. I recalled the stories I had heard. They agreed on one thing: the silver is still down there. As the miners got down to the mine's depths, they carved pillars and roofs out of almost solid silver. But if anyone were to take out the roof or a pillar of silver, the mine would crash down on them. Water rushing in would finish the job. And them.

Scuba divers are not allowed down there, but some went anyway. One diving team descended the main shaft and swam into one of the side tunnels, until they came to fallen timbers blocking their way.

"I got part way through several timbers but then stopped," a diver said. "They felt a little loose to me. You realize that if you dislodge one, the whole works can come crashing down on your head. Underwater, that kind of makes you think."

It made him thoughtful enough to turn around and leave.

Silver Islet is privately owned; visitors are discouraged from stepping on its rocky shores. But visitors can find their way to the mine entryway.

No gates, locks, or steel bars guard the mine. The entryway is only an uncovered hole.

But that's filled with water. The guard is Superior.

.... ❈ ....

At sunset, a chill wind blew through the old mining town. I turned on the VHF to the Canadian weather channel. "Small craft warning," it reported. "Winds in the east, increasing to 40 knots, becoming southeasterly."

Forty knots of wind would kick up sizeable waves. But I was inside the break wall at the government dock. I would be OK.

I snapped off the radio and glanced about. There was a sturdy break wall, but I saw the entryway itself was wide open to anything from the east or southeast.

On impulse, I picked up my hand compass. The lubber line swung to the southeast. I realized I'd catch anything that rolled in through that open entryway.

As a trace of wind started to moan in the rigging, I recalled one sailor's warning: he told me that the most miserable night he'd spent anywhere at a dock was at Silver Islet. "It's wide open to storms from the east."

.... ❀ ....

It built with a low moan, then a howl. The boat began rocking back and forth as waves rolled in. The harbor and the water became black with the storm. I heard the awful noise of the wind on the mast and in the rigging. Gear and cans of provisions inside my boat clanked and moved about.

Moan. Shudder. Thump. My little boat was getting lifted and slammed into the fenders, twisting back and forth. We were in a deadly dance with the wind and waves, the mast swinging one way, then another, fenders groaning. The hull was moving up and down.

Clank. Slam. Groan. My boat was catching every gust, lifting to every wave peak, dropping into every trough. The motion increased as the storm built.

I was fully dressed in my storm gear, including long johns and polar fleece, ready to leap out if an emergency flared up. I sat on my forward v-berth, on the starboard side, propping my back against the windward side of the cabin. I hoped my weight would ease the pounding. I was growing cold, so I pulled up my sleeping bag.

The darkness was awful. In the unlighted cabin, I could see nothing. Turning on my flashlight would only ruin my night vision. I thought of a solution: I turned on my ham-band radio. A tiny red diode glowed to show the long-range unit was powered up. It wasn't much light, but soon my eyes adjusted to the eerie red illumination.

In the constant motion, my ankle hurt. I got my injury from being dumped through the hatchway into the cabin by a storm a few days earlier. I braced it on a pile of clothing, but a dip and a slam against the piers, and the ankle would move. Pain would shoot up. No-aspirin aspirin only diminished the ache.

From time to time, I slid over to the portlight facing the dock. I shone my flashlight through the plastic. In the bouncing beam, I could see only inches away the hull working up and down and sideways against the camel.

I heard every sound, creak and groan. I felt the hull buck and lunge under me.

It was not a good night.

.... ❁ ....

About 1:30 a.m. I awoke, gasping. Somehow, I had managed to drowse off. I had slept fitfully, my mind conjuring up frightening thoughts.

"We're going under," one ghost had shouted. My body tensed, in full fight mode, adrenaline jolting my muscles. We were being swept under the pier and lay upside down in the water. Trapped. The chill waters reached up.

I was shaken. My heart pounding, I threw off the sleeping bag and grabbed for my flashlight. I checked the fenders, the camel, the lines once again. All were holding up so far.

In this storm, I could not move the boat. Nor could I leave the boat and sit up on that wind-swept dock. I had done everything I could.

I remembered that earlier, one of the kind old men of Silver Islet had invited me to spend the night in his cabin with he and his family. "It's going to be rough," he said. "Bring your sleeping bag up. You can throw it down in a corner."

I could be safe and warm away from the storm, in the comfort of a cabin. Instead, my choice was to stay with the boat, to protect it. I wanted to be here if anything went wrong, to do whatever I could. Whatever that might be.

I'd just have to ride it out.

Think positive thoughts, I told myself.

The image that my mind conjured up was that I was a boy once more lying in a lovely hammock. It was strung between two young trees. A breeze had come up, and the trees swayed in the wind. With it, the hammock rocked back and foth. It was a pleasant motion, in my mind at least.

I fell asleep, my flashlight in hand, shivering in the chill, as my boat bashed against the dock.

.... �֍ ....

At first light, I awakened. All had changed. I looked out at the harbor. It was gray out there and I could see dark waters tipped with whitecaps rolling in. We still bounced around, creaking at the dock against the fenders and the camel. But it was different now. Calmer.

I checked myself in the small mirror and winced. A haggard, white reflection looked back. I could see shadows under my eyes from lack of sleep. I had aged years. But I had survived a terrible night.

Still shivering in my long underwear, polar fleece and heavy boot socks, I carefully pulled open the hatch. A patter of rain greeted me as I stuck my head outside. It was a dark, wet day. I climbed up on the old dock and raised my body upright, working out the kinks in my body. I'd felt crappy before, but now it seemed as if my entire body was a mass of hurt and bruises.

A cheerful dock worker greeted me. "Another gray day," he said. "Might as well get used to it up here."

"Thanks. I'm adjusting." I ambled off the wet dock and pointed my deck shoes onto the wetter land. Above me, to the north loomed the giant mountain of legend, the Sleeping Giant. At water's edge was the sleepy little hamlet of Silver Islet.

Stretching my legs was helping. I began to feel better as I hobbled uphill to the main street. I took in a deep breath of fresh air coming from the big lake. It was refreshing.

Tomorrow, when the weather cleared a bit, we'd shove off again. I started to get back my sense of adventure. We had already survived the longest night I'd ever spent. My boat and I had been on an elevator, going up, then slamming down, then bumping sideways, and sometimes going both ways at once.

My spirits began to rise.

I congratulated myself: We had survived another adventure. Daylight brought not only brightness and warmth but a new faith in my boat and myself. �֍

20

The tale of The Essex

Broken bones tell an amazing story

SLIPPING ON MY DIVING MASK AND SNORKEL, I lay down in the water to peer at the old timbers. The front part of the wreck was almost on the beach, and the old vessel extended out in the sloping water. At the end, it was covered by about four feet of water.

I floated motionless, gazing downward, fascinated. What a sight! Though blackened, these were remnants of a large wind ship.

Something gleamed in the water. Swimming closer, I saw it was a copper bolt, lying underneath part of the heavy wood structure. I wondered what it was for: something that held part of the old vessel's inner structure together? It was an inch in diameter and about a foot long, fitted with what looked like several washers at one end. The end was thicker than the washers, and it appeared to have been pounded over. I later learned that this was a drift bolt, with cinch rings.

This wreck was all that was left of the *U.S.S. Essex*, built over a hundred and fifty years ago. She was once a proud Naval ship that had ranged the world. The *Essex* is one of the last vessels built by Donald McKay, the American master builder of clipper ships that set so many oceans-going records.

The once proud sloop of war had not died in battle. The *Essex* had been deliberately burned, sunk and left to rot in the shallow waters near Duluth.

.... ❁ ....

As a boy, I spent countless hours building a model of the most famous clipper of them all, *Flying Cloud* (built 1851, extreme clipper, 1782 tons). In 1854, she set the world's record of 89 days 8 hours around Cape Horn from New York to San Francisco. This was a record under sail broken only in recent years by a modern racing sailboat. McKay's clipper was fully loaded with passengers and hundreds of tons of cargo. The modern sailboat was stripped out to race.

McKay's other clippers, now lost along with *Flying Cloud*, bore names that ring with romance and adventure: *Sovereign of the Seas* (1852, extreme clipper, 2421 tons), and *Stag Hound* (1850, extreme clipper, 1534 tons). McKay's clippers set records for long-distance speed unequaled in their time: over 400 miles in a day. His *Champion of the Seas* (1854, clipper, 2447 tons), achieved a single day's run of 465 miles, a record that has never been broken for a cargo carrying vessel under sail. They were legends when sail was in its greatest glory. They gloried in heavy weather sailing: The *Flying Cloud* had exceptional speed in storms.

Only two of McKay's vessels outlived him. The *Essex*, whose bones now lie off the Minnesota Point, and, the *Glory of the Seas* (1869, a medium clipper, 2102 tons), which spent her last years in Puget Sound as a floating fish storage plant. She was towed ashore in 1923 on a beach near Fauntleroy, Washington, where she was burned for her copper metals and other fastenings.

From the underwater bones of the last surviving McKay ship, I could only get an idea of the story that the Essex represented. She was history, a sister to *Flying Cloud* from the same master's hands. As I touched her timbers, I used my imagination to summon up visions of the fine old ship. How she must have appeared, years ago, her decks awash, her tall spires and rigging groaning in the storms; a white cloud of sails slamming her hull through the world's wild seas.

.... ❁ ....

The *Essex* was a naval sloop of war, a three-masted sailing machine but with a 1,200-horsepower steam powered auxiliary engine turning a single screw. She was commissioned on October 3, 1876. Displacing

1,375 tons, the *Essex* was 185 feet long, had a 35 foot beam and drew 14 feet, three inches. As an Enterprise-class vessel, she carried four smooth bored 9-inch guns, one 11-inch gun, and one 5 inch muzzleloader. Like other vessels of her day, the warship carried a full set of sails and relied on her sail power for ocean voyaging.

The McKay heritage was unmistakable in the jut of her clipper type bow, long bowsprit and fine entry. Her tall masts ranged skyward from her wooden deck, and, aside from a tall, black smoke funnel between fore and mainmast, she looked like a sailing ship from the heyday of America's great square-riggers. She was one of the last sail powered fighting ships built of wood for the U.S. Navy.

Regarded as one of the finest ships of the fleet, she was first assigned to the North Atlantic, then later, the South Atlantic Squadron. She cruised to Liberia and along the west coast of Africa. From 1881 to 1882, she sailed the Pacific; in 1883, she became part of the Asiatic Squadron, when she protected missionaries at Ponapai, Caroline Islands, during a native uprising. She was in Manila Bay in Cuba when the *U.S.S. Maine* was sunk; she was sent on a relief mission when Admiral Perry discovered the North Pole.

After about 27 years of active service (1876—1903), she left her salt-water environment to sail the Great Lakes, first in Ohio where she served for 12 years in the naval reserves. By 1927, she was berthed in Duluth, Minnesota, for training duties with the Naval Reserve of the State of Minnesota. By this time, she was an old ship and they didn't do much maintenance on her. The naval reserve built a shed atop her deck and made her into a floating naval receiving ship in Superior harbor. She was taken off the Navy list in 1930.

The *Essex* by this time was the last McKay vessel afloat. She was also the oldest steam powered vessel in the navy and its last wooden hulled sloop of war. She had outlived all other vessels in her class by over 11 years. The news of her scrapping led the Detroit Free Press to write: "initial steps to divorce her from the navy will be instituted when she is offered to the highest bidder adjudged capable of treating her kindly in her old age."

She was sold for $410 to the Klatzky Iron and Metal Company. On October 13, 1931, they towed the 55 year-old *Essex* out of Superior harbor to Minnesota Point's lake side. The last McKay vessel was lashed with a steel cable around each side and doused with 200 gallons of kerosene and oil. They set her on fire.

An eyewitness account in the Evening Telegram, Superior, Wisconsin, reported on her fiery death:

"Most of the good oaken ship *USS Essex*, once one of the finest vessels in the United States fleet, was being scattered over Lake Superior Thursday in the form of charred bits of wood. There were no ceremonies to mark the *Essex's* end. Even the American flag, ever conspicuous during her naval and naval militia days, was lacking. The burning of the grand old ship of the line was supervised by the United States government, which gave orders that nothing be left in the lake to menace navigation."

She blazed through the day and the night. After she burned to the waterline, the salvagers hooked up the steel cables and winched her onto the beach. Salvagers tore through her blackened bones for copper and bronze spikes and bolts.

What was left of the *Essex* remained in Superior's shallow waters, pounded by surf and encrusted by ice. From time to time, amateur salvagers and souvenir seekers used chainsaws, hacksaws, pry bars and axes to get more drift pins and bolts.

Some sawed her bones to get firewood for a beach party.

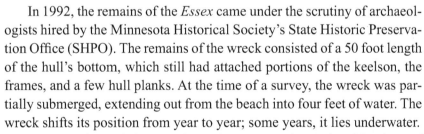

In 1992, the remains of the *Essex* came under the scrutiny of archaeologists hired by the Minnesota Historical Society's State Historic Preservation Office (SHPO). The remains of the wreck consisted of a 50 foot length of the hull's bottom, which still had attached portions of the keelson, the frames, and a few hull planks. At the time of a survey, the wreck was partially submerged, extending out from the beach into four feet of water. The wreck shifts its position from year to year; some years, it lies underwater.

But enough was left to nominate the *Essex* to the National Register of Historic Places. Scott Anfinson, of SHPO, who worked on the early efforts on behalf of the *Essex*, told me that the nomination was justified because the wreck could still be used to document construction methods on mid 19th century naval vessels. The *U.S.S. Essex's* wreck was placed on the National Register on April 14, 1994.

"It's an artifact of history like no other in Minnesota," he said. "Go and touch a piece of his work; you can't do that any place else." He emphasized, "Naval archaeologists say you can still see the master work in the wood. This was a person who knew wooden ships."

"When I go there," he said, "I always feel a sense of wonder that these few fragments speak to me. I can visualize the complete vessel with its tall masts, yards and arms. Every time I talk about it, I get choked up. Something about the *Essex* gets to me."

.... ※ ....

The day was bright and clear as I once again made my way along the sandy beaches of the Minnesota Point to the Superior entryway. Out on Superior's blue waters, a few fishermen bobbed in small boats. Even in mid-May, I saw black patches in the golden sands. They were ice chunks that had not yet melted.

I was on my annual pilgrimage to the old ship.

Would she make an appearance this year, poking her old blackened bones above the sand? Or would she remain hidden, as she has for several years, and not permit a peek of what was once her great glory and heritage?

Searching for her, I walked back and forth on the beach. This year she was not to be seen. Perhaps she was slumbering or resting under the sands.

Another thought came to me: Perhaps she was hiding in shame. ※

21

The secrets of the island

Courage lives on Madeline Island

MY BOW WAS LIFTING WITH THE WAVES, smashing out sheets of spray. The high winds of last night, coupled with today's 40-knot breezes, had kicked up steep wave trains. I was sailing right into them.

I sat back in the cockpit, one hand on the tiller, the other bracing myself. Despite all the bucking, I felt exhilarated and secure. The bow would throw up spray as each wave rolled toward us. We'd climb over and then—whump! The stern would fly in the air. It was like being on a teeter totter.

As I neared Madeline Island, I headed into the wind to drop my mainsail and furl my jib. I cruised under power through the channel, past the old Chippewa burial ground, and into the inner harbor.

I had landed on one of the most unusual and historic islands in America.

Madeline is the only island on Lake Superior that is inhabited year-around. Though it swells with thousands of tourists and residents in the summer, the population shrinks to a hundred hardy people who live there year around. They lead a rugged life: islanders face storms in the fall and winters when the big lake freezes over and isolates them.

The island has lived under three flags—French, English, and American. It was from this island that birch-bark canoes explored much of Lake Superior. Madeline was home to voyageurs.

Idyllic, I thought. But I remembered the words of Nori Newago, who spent most of her life on the island and was chairman of Madeline's only town, LaPoint: "Sometimes we feel like we are still pioneering, challenged all the time. Everything we do is dictated by Superior. You have to respect it and you can't take chances. Nearly everyone on the island has had someone who died on the lake—my mother was drowned on it."

Before any white men, the island had the Chippewa, who came from the east at about the same time as Columbus came to this continent. It was a peaceful life on Madeline at first, but after a few centuries there were too many people on this small island, probably as many as ten thousand; they began to die of starvation. The legends say that they turned to cannibalism and the medicine men began eating children. The tribe was horrified and killed their spiritual leaders. Madeline became haunted. The tribe could hear the spirits of the dead walking the island at night; they saw globes of fire dancing on the marshes. Everyone became afraid. The Chippewa left the island and did not return for about two hundred years.

"Even then," Nori said, "for many years after, none of the tribe liked to spend an evening on the island."

······················ ❁ ····················

Off to one side, near to an open shed, I could see animal pelts stretched on frames to dry. A deer skull with antlers was suspended in a tree; I had the distinct feeling I had stepped back in time a couple of hundred years to an early trapper's cabin. I knew this was the home of The Digger, a man who had learned more about the island's history than anyone.

A white-haired man, looking much like an oversized woods gnome dressed in weathered green shirt and pants, opened the doorway, blinking in the sunlight.

"Come in, come in," Al Galazen said.

On the walls hung a collection worthy of a museum, artifacts from the earliest days of America: flint arrowheads, axes and knives of stone, birchbark weavings, pieces of rusted French muskets, and small, personal ornaments from the Chippewa, the French, the English and the early American settlers.

"My wallpaper." He motioned with his hands. "I dug it up and I dig whenever I get the chance. And that is, just about every day."

He rummaged through various drawers, boxes, and cabinets. Out came rusted revolvers, knives, belt buckles and buttons from French and

English uniforms.

"How do you know where to dig?"

"The earth tells me," he said. "I learned the trick from an old grave digger. This is how you find old graves. I take my long rod and I insert it in the earth. I can tell a lot by how it feels, whether or not the earth has been disturbed."

I wondered how far back he could "feel" the earth.

"For as far back as a thousand years. If my rod squeaks, the earth has not been disturbed."

"How do you find places to dig?"

"You have to look: a compression in the earth, something in the woods that is the wrong size, or even rocks out of place. That's the place to go"

He began to reminisce as he rocked in his old wooden chair. "I was born in 1903 in Superior and I came to the islands over fifty years ago. I figured if it was good enough for the fish, it was good enough for me.

"When I feel like it, I just get my rod and disappear for a while. Sometimes I dig in the earth, watching for the color of the dirt as I dig. When it turns black, I started digging carefully. Those are ashes from an old campfire.

"Sometimes I put waders on and dig underwater. Since about the year 1400, the island has changed a lot and some old campsites are underwater at Grant's Point. So long as you can see the black stuff coming up, you know you're on an old campground. I find a lot of pottery that way and rolls of birchbark. Indians and Voyageurs used the birchbark to repair the skin of their canoes. They used to cook in it, too.

"I found war paint once, gray and red color in birchbark containers. It's made of roots, stone, and bear grease. You put it on your fingers today and you can hardly get it off. It's still good after a hundred and fifty years."

He poked around in an old box he had pulled from under a dresser.

"And here's my watchman!" He withdrew a human skull for me to admire. "I dug him up. That's a bullet hole. I date the skull from the late 1700s, and from the uniform remains, he was a British soldier. I'd guess his age to be about thirty-five."

"He's your watchman?" I gingerly held up the skull.

"Whenever I go away, I just put him out in the middle of the floor. If anybody breaks in here, they'll see my watchman and get scared off."

"Does it work?"

"Nobody's taken anything yet." He smiled.

.... ❀ ....

I walked down the island's main street of its only town, LaPoint. Downtown was a collection of one-and two-story wood frame buildings of intermediate age and construction, arising around a focal point, a grocery store, a gas station, a restaurant and a bar.

I was wondering what to do next on my on-foot exploration when I saw a patrol car, so I waved at it. The patrolmen slowed beside me and rolled down his window.

"My name's Marlin Bree," I said. "I'd like to talk with you."

"Okay," he said.

"I sailed in yesterday. I've got that wooden sailboat in Three-C."

He brightened. "The little varnished one?"

"Right. I spent seven years building it and I'm sailing Superior this summer. Can I ride with you for a while?"

He shrugged. "Hop in."

That was my introduction to Patrolman Jim Cook, a friendly and stout-looking young man.

On the waterfront, my boat was my ticket to meeting people. When I first started sailing, I thought people would look down their noses at my 20-foot wooden boat, but matters turned out just the opposite. They could see the time, effort and thinking I had put into my little cruiser. If my boat was Ok, then so was I. My boat was introducing me.

As he drove, he told me patrolling the island from tip to tip over all its twisty roads was fifty-two miles and takes less than two hours, without hurrying.

"How long does it take to drive through downtown?"

"About two minutes. But I haven't been bored yet and I've been here since September."

"Any crime on the island? I notice the islanders don't lock their doors when they go out."

"Think about it. This is an island. What can you steal large enough to make you money that you can carry across on the ferry? Once there were some motorcycle gangs up from the Cities and they were ready for trouble.

I had to tell them not to hit me for their own good."

"Did that work?"

"They got the message. They realized that they were isolated here. There's nowhere to go that they can't be found. So where can they run?"

We were now completing the sweep of the island to north and heading along the eastern shore. Through the trees, I could see what looked like the tail of a small aircraft. As we came nearer, I could see wings. Atop the plane, the American flag flew. It looked like a World War I fighter had crashed.

"Oh, that," Patrolman Cook said. "That's the Red Baron's plane."

"I gotta meet him sometime."

"Hurry. He takes an awful lot of chances."

.... ※ ....

The Red Baron was an intense young man in his late twenties. Despite the chill air, he wore a light shirt, jeans and tattered sneakers. Wayne Nelson sniffed the air like a sailor, then felt it on his face. "It's a little breezy today, gusting up to about thirty-five knots. Up here, if you want to fly, you fly."

I looked closer at his plane. *Beaufort T* was a rag job: fabric covered its wings and tail, but the rest was exposed aluminum tubing. The wing was high, and on top was a strut with wires, much like an old-fashioned biplane bracing. Below the wing was slung a pod, with its engine, a modified snowmobile motor, in the back. In the front was the single pilot's seat.

"I've been flying planes since I was old enough to sit on my dad's lap, so I've spent a lot of time in the air. I love flying. But more than that, it's one salvation of my sanity. When the world gets to be too much for me, I go up in the sky."

I mentioned, seagulls.

"Somebody's been talking," the Baron said. "But it's true that I catch seagulls."

"Ducks are much too fast and so are cormorants. But seagulls fly at about forty-five miles per hour and that's about right for me and *Beaufort T*. You come up from behind them as they fly along. When you get within fifty feet, they'll start getting nervous and turn their heads, and you'll see those black eyes on you, wondering what you will do. Oh, they'll try a fake maneuver, trying to throw you off, because they're smart birds. But once they discover you're as smart as they are, the duel begins."

He stretched his arms wide apart and began to imitate flight patterns of the seagull.

"They'll keep turning their heads around, watching you, because they figure you're another bird. So, when they see you lift one wing, they'll figure you're going one way, and they'll head the other way."

With his arms upswept, the Baron swung down and around.

"So, what you do is you fake them out with a quick little wing lift," he said, shifting his arms. "When they turn the other way, you turn with them on the inside. Then you've got them." He stood upright, his eyes gleaming.

"You catch them?"

"Oh, no! Nothing like that. That might hurt the bird. What you do is you touch wings with them, and just kind of catch them. Doesn't hurt them at all, except their tail feathers go out and up and it's undignified. They look silly. It hurts their pride."

"Then?"

"Oh. I hold them there on my wing for a few seconds, then edge off on my throttle, and off they fly." He grinned. "My dog likes that, too."

"You take your dog up?" His dog was part wolf, already weighed over 100 pounds, and was not yet fully grown.

"You can if you tuck him in between your legs. Just his head sticks out. He loves it."

I imagined the two of them, the young flyer and the wolfhound with his ears flapping in the breeze, sailing over the islands.

He flew year-round, both because he was in charge of the island's ice road, and just for fun.

"It's not awfully cold up there," he explained. "an ultralight only goes thirty-four to forty miles per hour and because *Beauford T* has a pod, the wind goes around you. I wear a ski mask, full helmet, chopper gloves, and a snowmobile suit.

"A little airplane like this is very handy in winter. I can fly out over the ice and check its condition, look for lost snowmobilers, and for cars that have broken through the ice—all sort of things."

Just months before, in the dead of winter, the Coast Guard had called the Baron at midnight. A fishing boat from Red Cliff, the *Energy,* had been caught beside Devil's Island—the outermost of the Apostles—in an ice jam up. Could he help?

The next morning, he flew to the Bayfield Coast Guard Station and landed his plane on the ice. But they told him that his volunteer services were no longer needed. They had called in a jet fighter to the rescue.

The Baron shook his head. "I decided to go out for myself and look. As I arrived over the island, I saw a Coast Guard jet throttle back to a hundred and fifty miles per hour, trying to assess the problem, but at that speed, he couldn't see much. Off in the distance, I could see the *Sundew*, the large Coast Guard boat out of Duluth."

"What did you do?"

"The ice was too rough for me to land on the frozen lake, so I found myself a landing place on Devil's Island. I came in over a fifty-foot cliff, landed, and walked as near as I could to the boat."

From his cliffside vantage point, the Baron hailed the *Energy*. The captain, Cecil Peterson, and his crew had been fishing when the ice moved in. It shoved the 40-foot boat up in the air 20 feet. There it perched, heeled over.

"I surprised the captain," the Baron said. "He told me he and his crew were all right but they were really hungry. I had seen some fishermen on my way out by North Twin Island. I turned *Beauford T* around, took off, and landed on the ice by the fishermen and explained Cecil's problem. They gave me three great big whitefish, and I dropped them down on the *Energy's* deck."

The Baron flew back to Madeline and talked with his brother, Arnie, who ran the island ice sled. The sled was the way the islanders got to and from the mainland when Superior iced up, since it could both glide across the ice and splash through open waters.

Arnie decided to go. The Baron warned him there was an ice maze going in, with ridges up to twelve feet high. Part of the way was glare ice; part was open water.

"The problem with the ice sled is that the only way to steer it is with power," the Baron explained. "But more power also means you are going faster, with less maneuverability, and there are no brakes. So, it got down to this: How could Arnie keep the sled going fast enough to maneuver through the maze of ice ridges?"

He scouted ahead in *Beauford T.*, with Arnie coming down the ice after him in the sled.

They worked out a system. "I'd fly along an expansion ridge and when I found a place where the ice sled could cross, I'd land and turn my plane around to show the right direction. Then, without slowing down, he'd roar past my nose

"After fifty or sixty takeoffs and landings, I had Arnie alongside the stranded fishing boat. I landed atop Devil's Island again and walked to the edge. I was just in time to hear Arnie's first words of greeting to the surprised crew."

"You ordered pizza?"

They had their first good laugh in days.

Their situation was dangerous. The fishing boat was up in the air, hoisted atop an ice floe. How could anyone get it down?

"The *Sundew* wanted the men off the boat, but Cecil and his crew didn't want to leave because the boat was their life. The *Sundew* didn't want to get too close, either, because the *Energy* could capsize.

"Arnie is an ice expert. In his ice boat, he swung back and forth along the ice ridge to examine the condition of the ice. The ridge was composed of individual cakes of ice. If pressure could be brought at a certain point, it might collapse.

"The *Sundew* nudged its steel bow into the ice; the ridge collapsed like a log pile. Down slid the Energy, right into the water. The whole operation took an hour and a half, maybe two."

The boats returned to harbor, and the Red Baron flew back to the island, landed in the snow, and pushed his aircraft back to its shelter behind the bushes.

I had to ask him: "Don't you ever worry?"

"Anyone who tells you he isn't afraid sometimes when he's flying or sailing is either stupid or a fool," he said. "Fear is always there, and that is not what is important. It's what you do with it that is. At times I feel like there are two of me. One person is saying, 'Stay back,' and the other is telling me, 'Meet the challenge.' I have been afraid many times. I don't see fear as the end of anything—it's merely a barrier to get across."

················· ❈ ·················

I was in the middle of the island at the center of a sand excavation pit, in a rusty steel building. "Well, there she is," Arnie Nelson said.

A machine hulked under a dusty tarpaulin. It was a squat, with large metal runners and an automobile wheel in front. In the back was a 250-hp. Army surplus tank engine, built in 1946. It swung a wooden propeller.

This was the island's homemade ice sled. It wouldn't win any beauty prizes

"This is our third sled," Arnie told me. "First, we had a wooden one, but that lasted only five years. It got wood fatigue from all the bending and twisting of getting in and out of the water. This aluminum one twists also but when it cracks, you just weld it back up."

I looked it over. The 20-foot hull was made of 3/8-inch-thick aluminum and rode on 6-inch-wide runners with stainless steel over them. Protruding out front, raised and lowered by a hydraulic jack, was an ungainly looking automobile tire used to help the machine get in and off the ice.

"You steer with rudders in the back. The ride is rough and nasty, but very fast. It's not easy to learn how to drive. Wind is a crucial factor—it likes to go sideways in the wind. The solution is more power and rudder. But when you do that, you go faster."

I wondered how he had learned to handle the beast. He smiled. "The first time I learned to drive was by getting in and going to Bayfield to pick up people."

"What's it like on a crossing?"

"Every trip is different, whether you're in deep snow, glare ice, or channel ice. Open water is the smoothest, but the passengers don't like it because we don't mind plunging right in. If people see the open water coming up, we try to give them a little encouragement to let them know this thing floats. I have had some people try to pay me double if I'd go slower. But I can't because we have a schedule to keep. Besides, it's cold out there.

"It's routine. We haul the school kids, passengers and mail, and everything we need on the island. The average crossing speed is about thirty miles per hour. That's on the ice and in and out of the water. But on glare ice, our speed builds up fast. I've had it over a hundred miles per hour, and at a hundred, it's a little scary.

"Sometimes we use it for rescue. We've gone out to fishermen caught in the ice packs and we have been down to Prairie du Chien, in Wisconsin, when we were hired by the hospital to haul doctors, nurses, and patients across the Mississippi. The bridge was out, and we roared back and forth around the clock. The rescues we don't like are when someone falls through the ice up here. There was a snowmobiler who was last seen on thin ice, and we couldn't find anything beyond where the tracks ended. We searched and divers went down under the ice, and there he was, in seventy feet of water right by his snowmobile. He must have had a heart attack."

There was a dark side: "Our fees barely pay for maintenance and if we broke down, who'd come to get us?"

He leaned back in the July sun. "People rely on us and it's our hobby to pick people off the ice. You could call this more or less of a service, but it's really part of the island."

······················ ❈ ······················

The island had a newspaper, *The Island Gazette* ($5 a year, circulation 600, no advertising.) Editor Sally Burke was born in the islands, spent much of her time as a fisherman's wife, and was now a widow in her mid-fifties. Her white-flecked hair was tied in two braids, which were coiled around her head. She was working on the newspaper's winter issue, which included a photo page about ice.

This season, two cars plunged to the bottom. "One car didn't stay on the ice trail and another one decided to take a shortcut and came too close to shore," she explained, adding that one car was a—she paused for proper emphasis—a Cadillac. "We're good at fishing out Cadillacs here."

The ice was serious business if you live on an island. "If it's too cold, the ice can get brittle. One car may get across, but it may create a crack for another car to break through. On the ice, it's best not to be second. And you never know if somebody has gone an hour ahead of you.

"Usually there is plenty of time before you're in trouble so you can get out—a wheel goes in and then the car gradually settles. If you are on real bad ice, though, there is no time—the car tips, and the weight pulls it down. I remember once I was on two solid feet of ice in a GMC pickup going to Bayfield for beer, but the temperature dropped. A heavy load had just gone across, a crack had formed, and somebody didn't know or didn't mark it. Our truck went onto the ice cake and began sliding into the water.

I opened the door to get out, and that was scary. If I had gotten off on the wrong side, I wouldn't be here today.

"But whether it's frozen or liquid, everybody who goes out on the lake gets caught sooner or later." She lowered her voice. "My grandfather lost his life sailing from Bayfield carrying the mail. He tried going across in April, when the ice was moving out, but the ice moved back in and capsized his little boat."

"Did you ever get caught?"

"Once we were in our boat *Dawn* on the north end of the island. The day was so still that not a leaf was blowing. But as we came around Steamboat Point, we ran right into a vicious storm. I was steering, and when my husband came back to the wheelhouse, his face had turned white. He took the wheel from me, but our boat was old and a little punky in the stern, and he was afraid to turn and run. So, he decided to face the storm. We must have had seventy-mile-an-hour winds; some waves were higher than our boat. There was no reason looking for life preservers, because you're better off remaining with the boat. It would probably stay up long enough to land somewhere, with you in it. We had a rough time, but eventually we made it back."

Her boat didn't survive all of Superior's storms.

"She was built in 'Thirty-nine, but went down in 'Forty-nine," Sally said. *Dawn* had sunk at anchor. A southwester had come up too fast and seas had broken in the gangway. She went underwater for two miles, then came up on a sandy beach. She was missing one whole side.

"They told my husband she was done for. But the *Dawn* was his life. So, he began working on her, despite everyone's advice. And in a while, she was back fishing for another thirty years."

A fifteen-minute ride along a bumpy gravel road in Sally's old car, and there was the *Dawn*, perched in a green meadow behind some pine trees.

"The kids put on a coat of paint now and then," Sally said. "to keep her up."

She walked to *Dawn's* side and ran her hand along the weathered planking. "She looks like hell now. But once she was nice.

Then Sally patted the little boat. "I think I'll just keep here right here. I figure she deserves a good resting place." ✸

Epilogue

-------------------------------★★★-----------------------------------

I HAD BEEN WARNED that others had entered this wild area and had disappeared. Neither they nor their boats were ever found. They told me I could get lost—or if I got into trouble, I would be on my own. It might be days before I'd see another boat or human being.

I was entering Lake Superior's most beautiful areas—and one of the sailing world's lesser-known places to cruise. It is a wild archipelago of freshwater, shoreline, and islands as unchanged as when the ancient Voyageurs paddled through in their birch-bark canoes.

For navigational aids, I relied on paper charts and my GPS. I was using Canadian Hydrographic Service chart 2301, Passage Island to Thunder Bay, with information both in English and French. Canadian charts give depths in fathoms, not feet; water less than three fathoms is tinted blue on the charts. Various tiny numbers dotted the blue areas, and, the detailed Canadian charts showed lots of blues where I intended to sail. That meant shallow waters or waters with reefs, some of them submerged.

A rugged cruising area—not for everyone.

I glanced at my GPS. We had picked up speed, recording 6.1 and touching 6.5 mph. I was getting my nav data from my GPS and ignoring my compasses for a good reason. To the north of me lay Magnet Island, and, on my chart, stamped in purple ink, was "Magnetic Disturbance/Anomalies magnetique." That meant my compasses could be off—all three of them. But my satellite stars for my GPS were true.

Waves smashed against my beam in small explosions of white. Dollops of foam slopped over the cockpit coaming, splashing me. I was flying along, getting help from the wind and waves. My GPS registered 6.9 mph. Outstanding for a 20-foot sailboat.

I flew into a channel, hoping to get some protection from the waves, but the wind had turned the channel between Spain and Gourdeau Island smoky. Brown tips of waves foamed off.

To enter Swede Harbor, I stood up in my cockpit. Now I could see further than if I were seated. With my Autohelm's remote control in my fist, I steered toward a place to tie up for the night. I shielded my eyes against the lowering sun. But first, I'd have to find the channel to a rustic dock.

My lower-unit depth finder was in operation; I could feel a slight shiver to the boat as the steel centerboard snicked against the bottom. The good news was that the centerboard depth sounder worked; the unwelcome news was I was in shallow water. I could see the bottom all too clearly.

I backed up, engine roaring in reverse. Then we moved ahead once more to find the channel several more times. In the final attempt, we succeed in running the bow aground on an underwater bank.

It was time to quit screwing around and go to Plan B, which was to get the hell out of there.

················ � ················

When I emerged past the northern tip of Swede Island, I caught the full brunt of the winds once again and encountered the smoky seas. Something was howling out here. I turned up the wick. Engine roaring, we soared past Rex Island, flew north along Spain Island, and then dashed along Lasher Island.

We needed to get off this lake. My cruising guide showed a small harbor inside an island. I ran along the edge of the island. Just when I thought I faced an unbroken wall of dark green pine trees, with their bases awash with waves, an almost unnoticeable channel opened up.

As I ducked in, the island took the brunt of the wind. Suddenly, it was calm. Outside my island, a savage windstorm raged. Here was sparkling clear water, riffled by zephyrs. I was home for the night in Loon Harbor.

I dropped two Danforths from the bow, one on each side, and, watched them sink in about 12 feet of clear water. They settled at an angle of about 20 degrees off each side of the bow. I always double anchor on Superior. Snicking the engine into reverse, I gave it the gun. Outboard roaring, prop churning up harbor water, the Danforths dug in. We didn't budge. We were secure for the night, riding at anchor.

I thought of supper. Perhaps a nice tin of Dinty Moore beef stew? That sounded good for a solo sailor. I could heat my meal on my single burner butane stove with very little fuss. Washing my utensils, a large bowl and a metal spoon, would not be difficult. All I had to do was stick it in the wilderness water and slosh it back and forth. Clean!

.... ❀ ....

The red sun goes down. I watch it drift across the length of my starboard portlight, then back again. The sun is not moving; my boat is. We are swinging at anchor.

I climb over the cabin top and move forward to the deck. It is still warm, the way wood holds its heat, and I lean back on the sloping forward cabin. Looking up, I scan the skies for the northern lights. I see them. They're up there, that eerie glow in the sky with moving streams of muted green, pale yellow, purple and red, weaving like a heavenly flag.

I am grateful. Superior is one of the precious few places left in the world where the atmosphere is clean enough to see an unobstructed night sky. That is important in the grand scheme of things. We're losing our pristine night skies; we're losing the night. And that is not all we're losing.

Thoughts come to mind. Some people feel the big lake's freshwaters are expendable relics, a leftover from another era, to be used up and polluted of at will. But to me, they are more important today than ever before.

Clean water is disappearing on our planet. As I sail Superior's open waters—well away from harbors and pollution—I can reach out my hand and scoop up a handful of drinkable fresh water. Coffee making in the morning is a ritual for me: using actual wilderness Superior water is my delight and a way to connect with nature.

But clean water is going fast: Superior is one of the few clean sources for drinking water in the world. Only 10 percent of the world's fresh water is drinkable.

We don't always understand what's happening, but we can sense the power of nature. Out here in the heart of the wilderness, I can feel nature's watery world envelop and restore me. Something elemental and profound is happening.

I am in motion. The world around me dances with light and shadows. I feel as if I had joined with some other, higher, and mighty thing. ❀

APPENDIX

PUBLICATIONS HISTORY

The old man and the inland sea. This chapter was originally published in slightly different form in Marlin Bree's book, *Broken Seas: True Tales of Extraordinary Seafaring Adventure*, and excerpted with permission and modified by *The Ensign* magazine, the publication of the United States Power Squadron. *The Ensign* version of the article (Jan/Feb 2007) won a First Place Award from Boating Writers International (BWI) and went on to compete for BWI's top writing award, the Grand Prize Award. Judged by instructors from Northwestern University's Medill School of Journalism, the article won BWI's coveted Grand Prize Award for 2008 for the author. Judging chair Jim Rhodes wrote: "The visual image of the old man frozen to his seat in the skiff, his head bowed, covered with frost, will stick with me a long time. After reading this story, I had to sit in front of a roaring fire at least an hour to get the chill out of my bones.") In a slightly different form, this Marlin Bree article published by *Lake Superior* magazine won a Bronze Award in the 2010 Best Feature Article competition of the Minnesota Magazine and Publishing Association. Also, the article won a 2010 Bronze award in the General Features category of International Regional Magazines Association.

Ship of dreams. This chapter was excerpted from Marlin Bree's book, *Call of the North Wind*, where it appeared as *The Long Voyage of the Homecoming* Ship, in slightly different and longer form.

Courage of the sole survivor. Excerpted and modified from Marlin Bree's book, *Wake of the Green Storm*. A portion of this material was excerpted and published as a magazine article by *The Ensign* (Sept/Oct 2008). It is a Second Place award winner for the author from BWI.

Warriors of the storm. This chapter was originally published in *Call of the North Wind* and excerpted as well as modified for this book. The material also was excerpted in May/June 2007 *The Ensign* magazine.

Ten feet across the Pacific. Excerpted and modified from Marlin Bree's *Broken Seas*. A portion of this chapter was excerpted by *Small Craft Advisor* under the title, *Yankee Girl*. Also, this material appeared in a slightly different form in the Spring 2011 issue of *The Ensign* magazine. The article won a First Place writing award from BWI.

The lost mariners. Excerpted and modified from Marlin Bree's *In the Teeth of the Northeaster*, where it appeared as the chapter, Up the Dark Shore.

Escape from the Island of Doom. Originally appeared in *Wake of the Green Storm* under the title, Lost in the Fog. Excerpted in slightly different form in Winter 2010 *The Ensign* magazine. Also, the article appeared in a slightly different form in *Small Craft Advisor* Magazine. Winner of a Third Place writing award for the author from Boating Writers International.

The last of the steam tugboats. Originally appeared in somewhat different form in Marlin Bree's book, *In the Teeth of the Northeaster*. Excerpted from the chapter, Up the Dark Shore.

The last battle of the Grampa Woo. Originally appeared in longer form in Marlin Bree's *Wake of the Green Storm*. Excerpted and modified in May/June 2009 *The Ensign* magazine. Winner of a First Place Award in Boating Writers Internationals Writing Contest.

The mystery ship from 19 fathoms. Originally published in Marlin Bree's book, *Broken Seas*, where it appeared as "The Lost Schooner: The incredible retrieval & loss of the 1846 *Alvin Clark*."

The Day Superior went wild. Originally published in longer form in the book, *Wake of the Green Storm*. Excerpted in the June 2015 *Minneapolis StarTribune* as "SUPERIOR'S FURY: Sailor recalls epic battle on the lake." An excerpted and modified article by the June 2003 *The Ensign* magazine, A Solo Sailor Meets his Storm of the Century, won a Grand Prize Writing Award for the author from Boating Writers International. Grand prize judges, who are associated with Northwestern University's Medill School of Journalism, described the article as "A real page turner. Compelling, engaging writing that is as fast moving as the storm that engulfed this sailor on what started off as a clear, calm day on Lake Superior. The writing is vivid in detail about what the sailor was seeing, feeling and thinking —all of that providing insights and lessons for others who could as easily find themselves in the eye of the storm."

The old shipwright of Thunder Bay. Originally appeared in longer form in Marlin Bree's *In the Teeth of the Northeaster*. An excerpt also appeared in *Small Craft Advisor* magazine.

Hard times on Bree's Reef. Originally appeared in somewhat different form in the book, *Wake of the Green Storm.* The material in modified form also appeared in *Small Craft Advisor* magazine.

The last hours of the Edmund Fitzgerald. Originally appeared in the book, *Broken Seas.* It also appeared in modified form in the *Duluth News Tribune* as, "The Big Fitz: controversy continues over what happened out there." Also, the material was reviewed by Don Boxmeyer of the *St. Paul Pioneer Press,* as "Tracing a Superior mystery: The final hours of the Fitz."

The legacy of the old fishing guide. Originally published in Marlin Bree's *Wake of the Green Storm.* Excerpted and modified in February 2003 *The Ensign* magazine.

The Mac comes back. Original magazine article first appeared in *Small Craft Advisor* magazine.

Midnight crossing. Excerpted from the book, *Wake of the Green Storm.* Also excerpted and modified in Sept/Oct 2007 *The Ensign* magazine. For this article, the author won a Third Place writing award.

The tale of the Essex. Originally appeared in Marlin Bree's book, *Call of the North Wind*, in the chapter, "An Homage to Two Wrecks."

The secrets of the island. Originally appeared in somewhat different form in the book, *In the Teeth of the Northeaster*, in the chapter, "Madeline: The Enchanted Island."

The awards and honors for the articles in this book are described and some are pictured on the author's website, **www.marlinbree.com**. Click on the category, Magazines.

Disclaimer

All reports are published for informational and educational purposes only, with no guarantees by the author or publisher. What works today might not work tomorrow for others, and it might not work forever for everyone. Individual judgment should prevail. Not responsible for liability or injuries, errors, and omissions.

Up from the depths, the 150-year-old *Alvin Clark* floats on her own bottom.
(See Mystery ship from 19 fathoms). Photo Dick Boyd

The old man and the inland sea

THE SUN WAS SLIDING BEHIND the Sawtooth Mountains as we picked our way down a woodsy trail that was knee-high in weeds. I was walking with Irene Malner and her husband on our way to Helmer Aakvik's old cabin. We came across it in a grassy clearing perched atop a rocky cliff overlooking Lake Superior.

The cabin stood close to nature. Here the winds swept off the lake; the Old Man could hear the splash of the surf on the rocks below. His view of Lake Superior was spectacular. As I came closer, I saw a pair of deer horns mounted above the front door to give this rustic, unpainted cabin a welcoming touch. The cabin had electricity, but no running water. Helmer's water supply was a bucket and the lake. He drank directly from Superior.

Nearby, a rocky outcrop overlooking Superior was where the fish house once stood. A three-log pole slide connected it with Superior below. After fishing on Lake Superior all day, Helmer had to winch his boat on the pole slide up the cliff to get it back to the fish house.

I wondered how he landed his boat during a storm. Irene told me that her father would time the waves, and on the seventh wave, he would power in at high speed and run the boat partway up the slide. He'd leap onto the slide, climb the poles to the boathouse and then winch the boat and its load of fish up the slide. It got more difficult in winter when the poles were icy.

It must have taken a special boat to handle all that. To me, boats are heroes and are a part of every sea saga. I wanted to find out more, but I was out of luck: Helmer's boat had been lost at sea. Weakened by Superior's wild storm, iced over and barely afloat, it sank when the Coast Guard tried to tow it back to Hovland.

Irene knew of a boat hidden away that was similar to the one in which her brother, Carl Hammer, lost his life. Helmer's boat was like the hidden boat, but older and punkier.

She took me to it. The North Shore skiff was workmanlike, functional, and very strong: its design was the evolution of years of fishing on Lake Superior in all its moods. The boat's unpainted, raw wood was gray with age. Up north, builders rarely painted wooden boats. Measuring 17 feet long, the boat had a 5-foot beam with a freeboard of 2 feet. The skiff was constructed of 17-foot-long pine boards 1-inch wide by 1½-inches deep.

One plank was nailed atop the other. For fastenings, Helmer built his craft with ordinary mild steel hardware store nails and screws, nothing fancy.

I asked Irene how heavy the boat was.

"Very," she answered.

A Superior fisherman could use his skiff for many years until it began to get punky. Then he would throw it away and venture into the North Woods where there was lots of boatbuilding wood and build a new one. Building time was swift: 3 to 4 weeks. Helmer's boat's age at the time of its disappearance was 20 years, which was old even by North Shore fishermen's standards.

Though Helmer had survived the deadly ice storm, "The Kid" was on everyone's minds. Carl had grown up in Hovland and worked in his family's fish house. Though the Old Man called him "the Kid," Carl was 26 years old, stood 6 feet tall, and had a strong, muscular frame.

"Our Carl....we missed him so much," a family member told me. "At sunset, we'd go out on the piers and look out over the lake and wait... maybe someday he'd just come sailing back to us. Or sometimes we'd see him in crowds. We'd look...there! It's Carl. Hey, Carl! But when we got close, nobody was there." She grew angry: "That damned lake!"

Up in the cemetery on a hill overlooking Superior, there's a grassy meadow, surrounded by pine trees. The wind off the lake rustles the branches. The Old Man is up there, beneath the earth in his wooden coffin built by a local boatbuilder, nothing fancy, but with a compass rose and a keel fitted on its bottom. But on another side of the cemetery are two graves....one is for Carl. No, he was never found. But there's a plot of earth up there for him and even a headstone. A family member explained: "Now we have him back with us, in a way. *He's home.*"

Ship of dreams

IF YOU EVER TRAVEL to western Minnesota, you will see among wooded acres a tall structure that looks like two huge white tents pitched end to end. This remote location near the banks of the Red River may seem like an unlikely place for a Viking ship to end its days. But as you enter the Heritage Hjemkomst Interpretive Center at Moorhead, you will find the homecoming ship, back from her memorable voyage from Lake Superior to Norway.

She gleams in golden wood, her mast towering up to the sail-like roof. A fierce dragon, the vessel's figurehead, rears high above the ship's bow as if surveying the dark seas ahead. War shields are hung along her rails, and near the water's edge, oar holes are open for rowers. The *Hjemkomst Viking Ship* is more than a memorial to one teacher's dream. It anchors and inspires a community where others can come to meet and to grow. And dream.

Thousands of visitors, including many school children, come to see this ship that the old boatbuilder Robert Asp constructed in a local potato warehouse. Some grow misty-eyed as they dream of the sea and the watery path to a distant homeland. They know, too, as they gaze upon the *Hjemkomst*, that a man's dreams can come true. The Old Boatbuilder's dreams did.

The last of the steam tugboats

AT 124-YEARS OF AGE, the historic steam tug *Edna G.* is in trouble. One day, volunteers found water in her bilge. A rivet head holding her thick steel plates had rusted off. A diver went in the water and stopped the leak with an epoxy patch.

Her old hull plates are thinning out; rivets are rusting. To keep her afloat, the 110-foot tug needs extensive repairs. That's a big problem for the Two Harbors community of 3,700 residents. They want her to continue as a water-borne museum, but repairs are estimated at $1 million. A news article in the *Minneapolis Star Tribune* pointed out, "Two Harbors struggles with saving beloved tug: Historic Edna G. tugboat needs costly repairs and maintenance."

They're working on the problem. A volunteer, Tom Koehler, said: "I have a feeling for this tug which is not rational, but you're talking about a boat here, so it doesn't have to be rational."

Courage of the sole survivor

THE SHIP BROKE APART AT THE SURFACE. The stern section of the *Morrell* sailed on and now lies on the bottom of Lake Huron in about 200 feet of water. She had traveled about five miles under her own power before sinking. The bow section sank where it broke in half and rests about 19 miles north of the tip of Michigan's thumb.

What happened for a modern ship to break in half? In its report, the Marine Board of Investigations speculated that the *Morrell* might have sustained a hull fracture.

This might have been caused because she was pounding into heavy seas or to struggling in them to maintain her heading. The board warned that any ballasted vessel of a design like the *Morrell* would suffer "severe stresses and strains in sea and wind conditions such as those present on 29 November should it remain in or at angles to the trough for any length of time."

The report concluded that a 600-foot vessel at an angle of 30 degrees to seas having crests of 250 to 300 feet apart "will suffer severe hogging, sagging and twisting stresses."

Such a tragedy could happen again if sea conditions are the same.

Survivor Dennis Hale added his own opinion: brittle steel. He said the *Morrell's* hull plates were designed with metal rated for maximum stress of 60,000 pounds per square inch. When a piece of the *Morrell's* hull was stress-tested, its steel tested fine at normal temperatures of 60 to 70 degrees. But when the temperature dropped to 35 to 40 degrees, the steel failed at 15,000 pounds per square inch—a huge drop in strength.

"So, it was brittle when cold," Dennis said.

The *Morrell* was built out of the same steel as another ship: the *Titanic*.

Dennis died at age 75 in 2015 from cancer. He was the lone survivor of one of the Great Lakes' most deadly shipwrecks. Dennis reflected on what he had been through: "I think somehow I give people a little hope in life, that life is a struggle, but if you have faith and determination, you can go through life and come out ahead."

Warriors of the storm

AS I SAILED IN THE CATAMARAN along the Shipwreck Coast, I became fascinated with a weathered building along a deserted shoreline. The men who worked there were remarkable mariners. They had a motto: You have to go out. You don't have to come back.

The Life Savers of Superior were the forerunners of today's Coast Guard. They went out in the worst weather that Superior could toss their way, summer and winter. Their long and light wooden boats were undecked and open to oncoming waves. Waves often swept on board and freezing spray would coat them. They got soaked to their skins in ice water; sometimes, they returned to shore frozen to their seats. Bystanders sometimes had to use axes to chop them out of the ice. They were frostbitten and half-frozen with inches of ice coating their clothing their equipment and their surfboat. They did their job and saved lives.

The Life Savers propelled their boats by long wooden oars. The captain steered their craft not with a conventional rudder but by an extra-long oar to give their boat more maneuverability in high waves.

They did not have waterproof clothing but wore oilies with a lot of wool underneath: wool underwear, wool pants and shirts, and sweaters. Wool would stay warm even when wet.

They were exceptional handlers of their small boats. In a storm, the Life Savers would try to get as close to the shipwreck as possible, often pulling their surfboat by hand along an ice-coated beach. They would launch their open wooden craft into the surf and row through heavy breakers to reach a stranded vessel, sometimes stranded on reefs.

Though their surf launches were dangerous and difficult, their return landings on storm-swept beaches were even more difficult. They returned to shore backward, with their bow to the sea, their transom facing the land. They rowed upon command between wave sets. Sometimes they deployed a canvas sea anchor that looked like a bucket. Trailing this drogue from the bow, the steersman with his long steering oar would attempt to hold the surfboat stern-to-shore in the waves. Should the boat get away from him, it could turn its beam to the waves, and capsize in the heavy surf. They lost many Life Savers in capsizes.

Those who survived deserved the title of "heroes of the surf."

Ten feet across the Pacific

GERRY SPIESS WAS AN INSPIRATION for those who loved the water and dreamed of having a boat but could not afford one. Little boats were his game—and he championed what they could do. For many small craft sailors, he was their inspiration and their hero.

The former Minnesota teacher crossed the North Atlantic, and later, the South Pacific, in his 10-foot long *Yankee Girl*. Both crossings became world records for the smallest craft to cross the biggest bodies of water. And an eye-opener.

"She's just like a nutshell, strong in every direction," he told me.

"How about capsizing?

"She'd just roll back up." Gerry had faith in his boat.

I worried about his engine. His outboard hung unprotected on the transom. During a storm, waves pounded the two-cycle Evinrude so hard that Gerry looked back "to see if it was still there." It was.

He had faith in his boat. Before his ocean voyages, he tested *Yankee Girl* in the worst weather he could find. As a violent storm descended, he motored into White Bear Lake. Buffeted by high winds, he inched forward atop the bouncing craft to raise the jib. Then he raised the main and put in a reef. *Yankee Girl* banged about in the storm gusts but survived.

Gerry believed you should never take a new boat on a voyage—only an old one. He had also tested himself: if he could not handle his craft in a storm on a small Minnesota lake, he'd never be able to do it on the North Atlantic.

When the little boat was on its trailer, Gerry invited me on board. *Yankee Girl* seemed almost commodious—a lot bigger than her 9 foot, 9-inch waterline would suggest. There was headroom. Stores were in hatches below my feet, out of the way. A single bunk ran along the starboard side so that a solo sailor could stretch out.

As problems popped up, Gerry continued to solve them. I saw Gerry down at the docks in Honolulu, cleaning out the bilges. "This is what saltwater will do," Gerry said, holding up rusted cans. The boat had shipped saltwater in the bilges during his stormy trip from California.

He removed water from his bilge with a meat baster and a sponge. It was not *Yankee Girl's* hatch that caused the problem: Gerry had jammed it shut using shims, including ball-point pens. The problem was a hole in the transom, where the stubby tiller entered the cabin. When Pacific waves slammed into the transom, spray came jetting in. His solution: a cloth gasket around the tiller that also fastened to the transom opening. Now he could move the tiller for steering, but no water came in.

"Permission to come aboard," I said. Gerry shook his head. "No."

I was puzzled, but I did not ask him again.

Somewhere at a mid-Pacific island, he relented. A KSTP-TV newsman was following *Yankee Girl's* progress, and Gerry said OK to Jason Davis' polite but insistent requests. Jason stepped on deck—and found himself swimming: *Yankee Girl* had thrown him into the harbor. Gerry had mastered the art of moving about his tippy little boat, but anyone else, including a seasoned newsman, was in jeopardy.

Gerry delighted in his ten-footer's sailing abilities. She could move on a broad reach, but most important, point high for a cruising sailboat, and, do both with steadiness and speed. Most cruising sailboats with their fin keels have about 45 degrees upwind (90 degrees both sides, combined). *Yankee Girl* could also point about 45 degrees, remarkable for such a small cruiser.

In the trade winds, he enjoyed his two-jib setup, his "two ponies." When set up for a downwind gallop, *Yankee Girl* could keep her on course by sheets (ropes) led from the jibs back to the cockpit and tied off with surgical tubing. He tensioned the elastic tubing so it would steer the boat. With his improvised self-steering, *Yankee Girl* could hit 100 miles a day, remarkable for a small craft. On her best day's run, she went 120 miles. Gerry could relax and let his boat sail herself. He sometimes groused that his boat could steer herself better than he could. But he got a lot of sleep.

Yankee Girl had a chine hull, rather than a rounded one, which Gerry felt was one key to her sailing abilities. "You could feel that chine dig in," he told me. The chined hull worked with her full keel. Gerry had experimented with several types and sizes of keels and decided his tiny boat needed a long keel, but not a deep one. It was a matter of balance: if *Yankee Girl's* keel were deep, such as a sailboat's fin keel, a large wave would overpower the small boat—make it trip over its own keel. *Yankee Girl* resulting keel was at its deepest only 3-inches. This stub keel gave her enough lateral resistance to make the boat point, but not vulnerable to cross-waves.

Yankee Girl's sailing abilities were due in part to her deep, large rudder with a bulb-like forward appendage. This "bulb" allowed the ply rudder to balance itself. Before the bulb, *Yankee Girl* had a hard helm and took a lot of effort to sail. But with a bulb counterbalancing the rudder, the helm became light, and steering was easier. Gerry felt it also helped her sail better.

Gerry's previous voyages showed him an offshore sailor needs a lot of protection from the elements. ("You don't go out there to rough it; you go out there to smooth it.") *Yankee Girl* doesn't have a cabin and an open cockpit, as most sailboats do. Instead, *Yankee Girl* is *all* cabin. Her cabin extends to the transom and has a large hatch cover—the cabin becomes the cockpit. He could handle his sails and steer from inside the cabin even with the hatch closed. He would be well protected from the elements.

To cross the world's largest ocean, he planned to sail, but when he could not sail, he would motor with his little fishing engine. He wanted to keep moving at all times, even in the doldrums. Gerry found he could run his outboard at fast idle day and night for days on end. Under low-rev engine power, and sipping gas, *Yankee Girl* covered 50 nautical miles per day. It was not fast, but Gerry did not want to go fast. He wanted to go far.

Gerry prepared himself for his long voyages. First, he "stuffed his mind" with positive thoughts. Underway, he had a goal: the end of the journey. Short term inconveniences did not deter him. His eyes were on the prize.

Gerry studied the problems of other solo sailors. Capt. Joshua Slocum, the first man to sail alone around the world, one day saw a seaman perched on his bow. "Steer to Port," the imaginary shipmate ordered. "We're almost there." Slocum recoiled in time: that course would have resulted in disaster. His imaginary and uninvited shipmate had become a problem.

Gerry brought along his own imaginary friend. He wanted one that he knew and trusted. So he invented one in advance. On his voyage, the imaginary friend turned up one day and became the sea companion Gerry needed. He was lonely no more. After he returned, Gerry did not talk much about his mysterious friend. When they neared the end of their journey, the imaginary friend vanished as mysteriously as when the friend had arrived. Gerry said he cried. He had become very attached. I never found out more.

One morning, I got telephone call. Gerry had been battling Parkinson's disease, but it still was devastating to hear that he was dead. Minnesota's marvelous solo sailor was gone forever

Before his death, he made provisions for his beloved boat. She now resides at the Minnesota Historical Society in Saint Paul. From time to time, *Yankee Girl* goes on exhibit in a special diorama showing her at sea. Her hatch is thrown open; visitors can peer below to see how Gerry lived when he was crossing oceans. Around the exhibit are passages from his book, *Alone Against the Atlantic*, so that others can catch his inspiration and share his dream.

He gave me a sextant he used onboard *Yankee Girl* on his Pacific voyage. Gerry carried several sextants and also carried a GPS. The GPS unit did not work very well for him, and he gave up on it. But the navigation aid he used was an inexpensive plastic sextant he bought for $30.

Gerry designed and built a larger version of *Yankee Girl*. At 15 feet, *Scooter* was to be the smallest boat that could carry two people around the world in safety and comfort. She sailed from Stillwater, Minnesota, down the Mississippi River to New Orleans, over the Gulf of Mexico to Florida. It was a challenging voyage: the Big Muddy was in dangerous floodwaters, and the advice to mariners was not to go. Undaunted, Gerry sailed southward with his sailing partner, Jackie Potts, sometimes perched on *Scooter's* bow with a boat hook, knocking deadheads out of the way. In Florida, they abandoned their around-the-world plans. Gerry told me he did not have it in him to sail further.

I wondered what happened to that boat. One day, driving down a rough country road, I was surprised when I glanced out at a large green pasture. In the center of the grass was a small blue-and-green boat sitting in an earthen berth, looking ready to sail on. *Scooter* was in her final resting place. There was no doubt I was at the home of Minnesota's master mariner.

Of his boats, *Yankee Girl* was his most beloved. She had carried him in safety and comfort across the biggest waters of the world. An ocean-crossing mariner paid her the highest compliment: *"Yankee Girl* was the last good small boat sailor. She could point, and she could reach. The rest are just downwind rafts."

The lost mariners

THE *BENJAMIN NOBLE* WAS LAST SEEN somewhere off the Duluth Canal heading for harbor when she disappeared with all hands on April 28, 1914.

Days later, her hatch covers washed up on the sandy beaches of Minnesota Point, along with her pilothouse. Life belts, a life raft, spars, oars, and clothing were scattered along Minnesota Point beaches and the shore about five miles from the harbor entryway. But her wreck was not found.

The four-year-old steel carrier was small at only 239 feet, with a beam of 40 feet. On her last voyage, an overzealous dock crew overloaded her with 2,900 tons of steel rails. Low in the water, she headed out of Two Harbors into an oncoming storm.

Some had seen the lights of a ship, and then there appeared to be two ships. A captain reported he had sighted the lights of a vessel fighting the seas, but the lights disappeared. When the storm cleared, the *Noble* was missing. The lost ship became Superior's ghost ship.

In the fall of 2004, Jerry Eliason, Kraig Smith, Ken Merryman, and Randy Beebe were searching for a shipwreck when their boat's side-scan sonar picked up something: a ship below them. It was the *Noble*, on the bottom near Knife River, about 20 miles from Duluth.

Diver Jerry Eliason reported that it was one of the strangest wrecks he'd ever been on: the front half lay buried in about 50 feet of mud. Overloaded, the *Noble* was "a submarine waiting to happen." A large wave boarded the ship, weighed the bow down, and the *Noble* submarined into the bottom with enough speed to carve a 50-foot deep crater in the clay bottom.

No one survived. Nor was there any report from the ship in its final hours.

One day, a boy walking along the Minnesota Point found a bottle with a note inside: "God! S.O.S. God help us. On board the ill-fated steamer; is doomed tonight. God S.O.S. Goodbye everybody."

It was thought to have been written by someone aboard the *Noble* during its last hours.

Escape from the Island of Doom

AN OLD PHOTOGRAPH CAUGHT MY EYE. Dramatically, it showed a beautiful ship with its bow sticking up out of the water, teetering on a rock.

"That's the *Guinilda*," Ned Basher said.

I was at the old Rossport Inn in Rossport Harbor, one of the area's most picturesque harbors, where I tied up after my voyage past the Island of Doom.

In August 1911, the *Guinilda* was steaming in these wild Canadian waters on its way to Rossport. The vessel was the pride of wealthy William L. Harkness, one of the original partners of Standard Oil. But Harkness would not hire a local pilot at the cost of $25 to guide his yacht through rock-filled waters. The millionaire ordered his captain to steam ahead.

The 195-foot yacht rammed her keel on a hidden reef. At speed, her hull slid forward on the reef and ended her forward progress when her entire bow was out of the water. Her bow was high, but her stern was close to the water. She teetered on the reef.

Harkness brought in a tugboat, but the cautious tug captain advised the millionaire to bring in two barges. The captain wanted to lash the barges, one on each side, to the Guinilda's stern. That would give her buoyancy.

Forget about the barges, Harkness said. He ordered the tug to pull his boat off without delay. When the *Guinilda* started to slide off, her stern went under—and kept going. She now sits in 250 feet of water without a hole in her. She is a boat with beautiful fittings, gold leaf on the bow, and even three grand pianos—a magnificent yacht in perfect condition. And only two years old.

What happened after Harkness watched his boat sink? Ned filled me in: He threw a lavish party at the Rossport Inn. "I suppose about all you can do after you sink a million-dollar yacht is get drunk and call Lloyds of London to tell them what they just lost."

"Must have been hard to lose that boat."

Harkness had the last word: "Don't worry," Harkness said. "They're still making yachts.'"

The last battle of the Grandpa Woo

MY CANPASS WAS READY so I could cross the border when I wanted, but Superior turned foggy and nasty. I waited stormbound.

I had a choice spot at Voyageur's Marina at Grand Portage, Minnesota, beside a rusty barge. Over the harbor's waters, I could barely see the stockade of an old fur fort and nearby Mount Josephine. This was where the ancient voyageurs had fought their way after their long paddle out of New France. The area was loaded with history.

It was also north country, I was reminded as I checked the thermometer inside my cabin: only 54 degrees. And this was early in July.

Nearby, the 65-foot aluminum-hulled excursion boat, the *Voyageur II*, was getting ready to make its run to Isle Royale. I heard the skipper advise passengers that there'd be a bumpy voyage today and that if they got sick, they should go to the fantail. "The worse place is the heads," he warned. He closed with a little north woods humor: "If you have questions, we'll try to answer them. If we don't know, we'll try to make something up."

The diesel engines roared, and off they sailed into the heavy fog, navigating on instruments. The sea was running in a dead roll—a motion that made people seasick. For some onboard, it would be an interesting voyage.

I met Kek Melby and Sue Johnson at Voyageur's Marina office. "That's where the *Woo* was moored," Kek told me, pointing to the waters off Grand Portage island about a mile away.

On July 4th, as the weather began to clear, the NOAA forecast was for the warmest day of the week—with storms predicted later in the day. But when I found myself on the open waters, a horrific storm overtook us. My boat was blown about like a toy, and her mast tip slammed down into the water. We fought downbursts estimated at 134 mph. I had found my first Derecho. Or rather, it had found me.

I fought my way into the tiny harbor of Thompson Island, chilled to the point of hypothermia and shaken by the awesome storm. On the island, as I warmed up, I met friendly Canadian boaters. Beside a roaring campfire, we talked about the lost *Grampa Woo*. These were waters that the *Woo* plied on her excursions. She often came into the island's harbor.

When the weather cleared, I sailed in a northern arc, moving from Thompson Island past T Harbor and into Siler Islet. From there, I sailed into the wildness islands. I realized I had sailed part of the route that the

Woo had followed that fateful night. This was where the Canadian tugboat and the Canadian Coast Guard vessel had attempted their rescue attempts. I could only imagine what they must have endured that stormy, snow-filled night. Sailing past T Harbor, I saw where they rammed their vessels' bows onto the beach, engines running to hold them in place against the storm.

After I finished my voyage, I got in touch with Capt. Dana on his cell phone. I had reached him when he was on board his *Grampa Woo II* headed south. He told me about his ordeal, starting with a surprise storm and his emergency drive to Grand Portage. Tethered to its mooring, *Grampa Woo* was holding firm. But she was without "wheels." Divers had removed the vessel's three propellers to prepare to install new ones that would arrive in a day. Despite high winds, the ship was riding the storm well. But then the deckhand yelled, "Captain, the *Grandpa Woo* is moving."

As Capt. Dana's sea story unfolded, I could reconstruct the *Woo's* voyage, Capt. Dana's experiences, and, interweave tales of the rescuers: the tugboat men and the coast guard people. It was a lengthy, complex process, working with e-mails and voice interviews. I continued my first-person interviews: I met Capt. Dawson of the rescue tugboat *Glenada* at a Gales of November diving conference in Duluth, when Clive Dudley, of Thunder Bay, brought him down from Canada.

Later, I was in Thunder Bay, Ontario, onboard the 76-foot harbor tugboat at the wheel where Capt. Dawson piloted his craft during the storm. As I peered out the *Glenada's* windshield, he told me how he could only see through a three-inch defrosted hole. He tapped the spot. He was looking for his deckhand Jim Harding, who was working on an iced-up deck. If the deckhand slipped into the stormy seas, he would have little chance of survival.

But Jim had pulled himself along a handrail to the wheelhouse and reached up with his wedding ring to tap the glass. Puzzled by the tapping, Capt. Dawson saw a hand waving outside the defrosted window. He yanked the pilothouse door open. Jim Harding, half-frozen and coated with ice, tumbled in.

As I walked along the deck, a door opened. I met the engineer on that heroic foray. He told me he had been on board the tug for years, but that storm was the first time he had felt seasick. He seemed a little abashed to admit it.

With a chuckle, Capt. Dana told me about "Oatmeal." During the storm, Capt. Dana was preparing to abandon ship when he noticed that his crew member Robin had disappeared. It was a desperate time: the winds were clocking out of the west at 90 mph., seas were roaring at 22 feet, and the boat's decks were awash with her topsides iced over.

He looked about, worried. Minutes later, the crewmember reappeared.

They went to the iced-over stern. When the harbor tug rammed the *Woo's* stern and held the position under power, Capt. Dana and Robin jumped down on the lunging bow of the *Glenada*. The deck was iced over; Capt. Dana recalls: "We slid on board, and as we slipped past the wheelhouse, we grabbed the door and crawled in."

Their rescuers fought their way to the minimal protection of T Harbor. They did not anchor on the leeward side but rammed their craft onto the beach at T Harbor. Both boats kept their engines running to keep their boats in place in the storm.

Belowdecks, the crews had donated dry clothing, and Dana and Robin stripped out of their wet clothing. As he undressed, Robin pulled a damp, brown-colored object from inside his jacket.

"What's that?" Capt. Dana asked.

"Oatmeal." Robin grinned.

Capt. Dana got the story: When they were abandoning ship, Robin went below to rescue the teddy bear. Oatmeal was a special memento of Robin's former girlfriend.

Capt. Dana made Oatmeal the third survivor of the *Woo*. He was given the berth of honor—near the wheelhouse's window—on the return trip when the new *Woo* came onto Superior. Together, they paid homage to the old *Woo's* underwater remains.

The *Glenada's* crew was awarded the Governor General's Medal of Bravery, one of the highest accolades Canada can give. The Thunder Bay Coast Guard crew received commendations for seamanship and bravery in what was described as "one of the most harrowing at-sea rescues in recent Great Lakes History."

The mystery ship from 19 fathoms

I FOUND THE OLD SCHOONER propped up in a dirt berth. Her waterfront museum was a fortress of plywood and scraps of timber. Unpainted, the *Clark* was weathered gray, her wooden hull strakes cracking. She sagged in the middle, with the ends uplifted. The hull had hogged.

I walked up to her weathered hull and put my hand on it. In the morning sun, it felt warm and comfortable. Wooden boats are like that. The old schooner was a treasure: not a replica, but a real boat snatched from a 150-year-old watery grave.

"She'll sail again." Diver Frank Huffman assured me. But it had been years since the divers had raised her.

As I went on board, the deck seemed springy beneath my deck shoes. In the aft cabin, the floor was not just springy; it was mushy—sure signs of rot. I reversed course and backed out. I had almost put my foot through the floor.

I tried to imagine what it was like to be at the helm of this huge craft. Just looking up at the masts and the 58-foot length of the boom put me in awe of the courage of the old-time schooner sailors. A waterfront adage came to mind: big schooners are killers.

As a museum draw, the *Clark* turned out to be a bust. Admiring crowds dwindled and almost stopped coming. No one seemed to know what to do with her. No museum wanted her—she was too big and would be too costly to maintain. Federal funds went to maintain other valuable historic vessels, but not the *Clark*.

Frank Hoffman and his team of volunteer sports divers had rescued this treasure from the depths at great sacrifice, with courage and persistence. Now she was rotting away on them.

She was also a mystery: there was no name on her or name board. The schooner had no identification number since that system did not begin until about 1855, long after they built the *Clark*. "This lack of identification is not a rare event with shipwrecks," Dr. Dick Boyd explained. "In my 50 years of diving I have been on many wrecks that held no identification of any kind and this was true for schooners and other small sailing vessels. I suspect this was because that data was painted on or put on boards, which were lost during the sinking. For whatever reason, nameless shipwrecks are common."

During the time the divers worked below, the sheriff's marine squads patrolled the site to ward off souvenir hunters and trespassing divers. It came as a surprise after the *Clark* was raised that several sport divers came to the museum, with a parcel or two under their arms or in the beds of their pickup trucks. Despite the heightened security, some divers had risked night descents and also dives during stormy weather to see the wreck and also to snatch a souvenir. Their return visits to the *Clark's* museum were their way of paying homage to the *Clark* and bringing back part of the lost schooner.

But who was "mystery ship?" Early newspaper reports on the *Clark* gave considerable detail and a precise location of the sinking. No other vessel matching that description had been lost in the vicinity and during that time. In the forward crew's quarters, volunteers found a small copper plate identified as a personal stencil that read: "Mich. Cray, Toronto, C.W." Dr. Boyd said: "Michael J. Cray was a survivor of the *Alvin Clark*. He was born in Toronto in 1843 and found his way to the United States, where he served one year in the Union Army during 1862 -1863, U.S. Army buttons were also found aboard the sunken vessel."

"Proof of identity was pretty much indirect and circumstantial," Dr. Boyd concluded. But they had established as well as they could that their vessel was the *Clark*.

Toward the end, the *Clark* flattened down, caving inward after her fastenings rusted through. Her keel cracked, and the vessel settled on her side. She was a disintegrating shambles of what she was when she was brought to the surface—the oldest and most significant wreck ever discovered on the Great Lakes.

In those days, the technology for saving old ships was not fully developed. Ships raised such as the *Vasa* in Sweden, or the *Mary Rose* in England had humidity-controlled buildings erected over them and sprayed with chemical preservatives. They were not left out in the weather to rot.

The *Clark* became the object of worldwide historical and naval archeological horror—a chilling and heart-rending example of what not to do when divers find a shipwreck. In 1987, Hoffman sold the *Clark* and the land on which she rested. The waterfront property had become prime real estate. The *Clark's* rotted timbers were no match for a bulldozer; she was broken up, shoved aside by the blade, and ground down under the heavy tracks. Big chunks were carted off and burned. Part of her still lies under the parking lot's asphalt.

If there was anything that came out of the tragedy, it was a study of what went wrong when old boats are recovered and brought to the surface. In 1987, the federal government enacted its Abandoned Shipwrecks Act, which regulates underwater archeology sites, claiming that an abandoned ship is the property of the state in which it lies. Divers may not remove any property, under penalty of law, nor may they raise the ship. The legislation was drafted after the sad experience of the *Alvin Clark*.

"It was a noble effort," Bernie Bloom told me, "and today not given its due." He paused a moment. "We had the ship. But where were all the experts when we needed them?"

The day Superior went wild

THE WIND SLAMMED THROUGH THE SHROUDS, beginning with a low moan, moving to a howl, then an ear-piercing shriek. Fighting to head my boat off in the wild winds, I jammed my tiller to port. Running with the wind, we sped up. *Persistence's* bow stuffed itself into a wave.

We stopped dead.

Headfirst, I flew out of the cockpit and slammed through the hatchway into the cabin below, ending with my feet above my head. A stabbing pain hit my right side. Glancing up, I saw my alarm clock fly in slow motion from one side of my cabin to the other side. My eyes followed: my starboard portlight had turned green.

The cabin's side was underwater. Capsize! I was in trouble.

Balancing on its side, *Persistence* teetered for a small eternity. I had a premonition: I was in the dark, trapped below in heart-stopping chill waters, and then swimming down to get out. I would have to clamber atop my overturned hull to hang on as long as I could while the storm carried me out into the middle of the lake.

Water sloshed up through the centerboard trunk. My boat reeled with every gust. *Persistence* tipped over so far that she seemed beyond the point of recovery. She teetered with her mast tip dipping in and out of the water. The tip rose a few feet, hung there, then slammed back down with another gust of wind. She would go only so far down, bounce, then fight to right herself. And then bounce again.

She was a fighting centerboard boat. Without a ballast keel, *Persistence* had no ton of lead at the tip of a fin keel to lever the boat back up. The sloop relied on the hull form for stability. This worked most of the time for small boats, except in extreme conditions. This was about as extreme as they get.

It was not my first rodeo. One windy day I was out with friends in my small day sailor, a center boarder. My friend, Frank, was handling the mainsheet. Despite my instructions, "Frank, let go!" he did not. His grip was frozen.

In slow motion, the boat immersed her starboard side. She lay for a moment with her mast flat on the water. I was surprised to see that her mast floated. It gurgled. Only when the air escaped, did the mast go down. It was taking on water. With its tip sinking below the waves, the boat turned turtle, the mast pointing toward the bottom. We laughed a bit—capsizes were not that uncommon in small sailboats—righted the boat, bailed out the water, and went back to sailing.

But I noted the buoyancy in the aluminum mast. Had the air stayed in, the boat would not have turned turtle. On *Persistence's* mast, I squirted in expanding foam sealant, first at the top and in various other places below. I figured that the hardened foam would prevent water from entering and the sealed air would give the mast buoyancy.

In the storm on Superior, *Persistence's* foamed mast dipped into the water, starting her death roll, but the sealed buoyancy in the mast levered the boat up. The mast's buoyancy had given my little boat her "bounce." The boat's righting motion took over.

Persistence had several ways to enhance her righting ability. Most little boats have rub rails of plastic or hard rubber along their hulls to take any bumps with docks or other boats. I built my rub rails out of 18-foot-long Sitka Spruce. The very light wood was about 1 inch thick, and I worked it in a tapered design about 2 inches deep at the bow and stern but broadening out to a little over 3 inches amidships. I epoxy coated the rails and covered them with 6-ounce fiberglass, which turned invisible after the epoxy coating. The golden wood rub rails take the brunt of the usual harbor bumps that a small boat is heir to.

But most importantly, they added righting motion to my little boat. These are like little wooden "life rafts" around the hull. In the storm, their buoyancy helped *Persistence* fight herself upright.

Taking a cue from Gerry Spiess's *Yankee Girl*, I built *Persistence's* cabin sides out nearly flush to the deck's edge. Unlike boats with cabin sides a foot or two distant from their hull sides, my boat has a cabin set-back of just 6 inches. This is enough space to incorporate a genoa track and ¾-inch square Sitka Spruce toe rails.

I can't walk around the boat, but I don't need to: I go up and over the cabin top. That rarely happens: my boat's jib is on roller furling. All controls, including those to the mainsail, get handled by sheets running back to me in the cockpit. I don't often need to go forward.

In her knockdown, my boat did not flop over on her side and keep going over, bottom up. Most small boats have stability up to when their rub rails are immersed before they flop over in an upside-down capsize. On my boat, the cabin sides become a buoyant part of the hull. When the starboard side of *Persistence's* cabin went underwater, and I saw green in the portlight, the submersed cabin was providing buoyancy and balance. We lay on our sides for several minutes, bouncing up and down. The buoyancy of the cabin sides, the rub rails, and the foamed mast all worked to keep us afloat. When the 100 miles-per-hour wind let up, the boat bounced upright. But it had been close.

I also took another cue from Gerry and built my cabin walls as strong and as thick as my hull. If the cabin ever went underwater, I figured, nothing would break. Nothing did.

After I returned to my home in Shoreview, Minnesota, I got the details of the full fury of the storm. News articles reported that winds had torn up a half a million acres of northern forests. About 25 million trees, including some old-growth northern pines, had been snapped like so many matchsticks, or turned over, their roots sticking up in the air. It was one of the largest North American forest disturbances in recorded history. Newspapers called it, "the storm of the century."

To get a first-hand look, I drove my old 4 x 4 through the devastated areas, once the forest roads were cleared of fallen trees. I saw not only tops of hills scraped bare but entire valleys scooped out of trees. I was awed.

One day I received an e-mail from a forecaster from NOAA's Storm Prediction Center, which was developing a website about derechos. I learned the July 4, 1999, "green storm" was a rare progressive derecho. Derechos (pronounced day–ray-cho) are violent, big superstorms produced by long-lived thunderstorm complexes. They barnstorm across regions with straight-line winds of 60 to 100 mph. Out of these high-speed thunderstorms ram downbursts and microbursts of heavy, chilly air. Slamming downward from squall lines, the winds hug the ground below, blasting anything in their path. NOAA reported that downburst winds are "well in excess and perhaps as much as double the gust front speed."

Meteorologist Paul Douglas, the *Minneapolis Star Tribune* weather columnist, said the Derecho that hit the northern area where I was sailing had winds as high as 134 mph. NOAA said that downbursts speed up on water since there is nothing to obstruct them, such as hills and forests. The deadly storms can come out of the sky anywhere over water or land and with very little warning.

They are "first worst" storms, with the most dangerous damage occurring during the first few minutes. One other scary fact: They can't be predicted.

I had been lucky. My boat was prepared for a storm but nothing like what we encountered. A thought came to mind. We worked hard. And the harder you work, the luckier you get.

The old shipwright from Thunder Bay

DOWN AT THE DOCKS in the harbor of Thunder Bay, Ontario, people are friendly and some stop by to chat and tell me the news. A singlehander had disappeared on the wild Canadian north shore where I had been exploring. One day, his white sloop was found shipwrecked on the rocks near Silver Islet, sails still set. But there was no trace of him. He was the second sailor lost this season in the wilderness area.

To the north of me, I saw an old wooden boat tie-up by a grassy embankment. It was the *Carioca*, owned by Albert Leon. He was returning to port from a voyage into the wilderness area and the Slate Islands.

Albert was the shipwright at Old Fort William, along an old Voyageur route on the Kaministikwia River, and a specialist in building old boats. In his boat shed, he took pride in working with antique hand tools to build replicas of the first boats on the lake.

Albert's masterpiece was a large schooner. The old shipwright had researched original plans of old sailing vessels to build her. The most difficult part in building the schooner was steaming the wood to make the curves. In the old days, Albert told me, the curves up front were so tight that just one knot in a plank could make it break. To gather wood to build his boat, he and his students and friends trudged into the nearby north woods to search for suitable white pine, spruce, birch, ash, elm, and tamarack. Crooks of tamarack were superb as ribs.

The schooner took seven years to build. He named it, *Persistence*. Tied to a pier at the old fur fort, the schooner was a majestic craft with a length of 60 feet, a beam of 17 feet, and a draft of 7 feet.

Down below, it surprised me to see daylight showing through what I expected to be tight-fitting hull planks. "That's the way they did it in the old days on the lake," Albert assured me. The wood would swell up. I walked on two planks laid atop the bottom ribs, which stuck above bilge water. I saw two Mercedes Benz marine diesel engines, just in case. He planned to take his schooner to visit ports on the Great Lakes on a goodwill mission.

A few years later, the Old Shipwright was depressed. The museum had sold his ship. "It was getting too expensive," he said. "They looked into their coffers and felt they could not justify the money to outfit and maintain a 60-foot schooner. So it had to go."

The Mac comes back

THE MAC GOT ITS NAME from Mackinac Island, in the Straits of Mackinac, on the old Voyageur canoe routes out of New France, Canada, to Grand Portage, Minnesota. In the late 1600s or the early 1700s, boat builders on Mackinac Island began building the Mackinaw design. By the 1830s, Mackinaws were popular and had become the 'pickup trucks' of the Great Lakes.

Commercial fishermen, fur trappers, copper miners, and island families sailed Mackinaw boats. A Mac carried the mail up and down the North Shore when there were no roads in the primitive wilderness areas of Superior. Mackinaws were well suited for Superior's boisterous conditions and small enough to be rowed or pulled up onshore.

Round-bottomed, Macs are 18 to 24-feet long and sailed by one or two sailors. They have a low freeboard but with an upswept, jaunty sheer and an enclosed, but short foredeck. Cockpits are open but protected with high coamings. In the old days, they built Macs outdoors near the water. Like canoes, Macs got constructed from the keel up.

The Mac I sailed, the *Paul La Plante,* had a typical symmetrical hull shape. Below the water, her hull is narrow at the bottom and gets wider near the waterline. This design makes her a speedy boat when she is empty and stable when loaded. The Mac carried ballast in the form of rocks that could be thrown overboard when the hull filled with cargo or fish. When I was aboard, it had 400 pounds of moveable lead ballast, but passengers and crew also could be pressed into service as moveable ballast. Without the lead, Cooper says, "she's awfully tender."

Mac's double-ended design had advantages. Its pointed stern worked well in following seas, which could bypass the boat without giving her transom a shove off course. A plumb bow dug in and worked well in the surf. It also gave the boat extra buoyancy, so the forward section did not bury.

The Mac also carried a lot of sail for a small boat. Her gaff rig spread sail low on the vessel (unlike the Bermuda rig). With her main and mizzen, the boat could balance off better than a single-mast rig: If a blow came up, the skipper could drop the mainsail and drive the boat on jib and mizzen only. A centerboard helped the vessel point well for its day and the stout, long keel gave it that "on the rails" feel that I admired when tracking in high seas. The Mac was a stable and easily helmed boat.

The *Paul LaPlante* was constructed from plans for an 18-foot version of the Mackinaw boat designed by Nelson Zimmer (*WoodenBoat* magazine: WB Plan No.14). Her hull is 18 feet, 8 inches long (not counting the rudder and bowsprit) with a beam of six feet. Her centerboard gives her pointing ability but lets her remain shoal-draft, drawing only 1 foot six inches (centerboard up) and 2 feet, 1 inch (centerboard down). Without added ballast, her weight is about 800 pounds, and she carries a sail area of 242 square feet, which is a lot. Her jib is spread out with a stubby little bowsprit, held down by a line (rope) rope bobstay.

The Mac has traditional wooden masts that handily lift out of their mast steps and can be stowed aboard. Sails are hanked on with hoops on the mast and laced with line to the booms and gaffs. The rudder is protected by a long keel and is secured with traditional gudgeons and pintails. Steering is done by tiller, with the helmsman sitting low, but forward of the sharp transom area, so that the boat has balance. The transom does not immerse and drag in the water to slow the boat.

Launched in June 2000, the replica Mac is hand-crafted of Minnesota North Shore materials: white oak for her keel, ribs and stem and sternpost, half-inch thick white pine for her planking, tamarack for her knees, and cedar for her decks. For spars, the boat builders selected standing, but dead, black spruce trees. Her mainmast is four inches in diameter and 18 feet, six inches in length, with the mizzen a little less. After experimenting with manila and hemp, the builders settled on running rigging of 3/8-inch diameter Dacron. North House volunteers made oars, manila fenders, and name boards. They also built her cleats and mast hoops.

At first, they coated her hull in a traditional Norwegian "boat soup" of pine tar, linseed oil, and turpentine. After some experience during the cool, foggy days on the North Shore, her builders replaced the long-drying "boat soup" with quick-drying Deks Olje for decks and seats; they put Sittkens Marine Cetol on the spars. Her trim is white enamel, and her bottom is red anti-fouling marine paint.

The Mackinaw boat was once the most highly regarded of small sail craft and widely used as a workhorse on Superior. Until the *Paul La Plante* was built, the Mackinaw had all but disappeared from Lake Superior. For restoring some of our marine heritage, we owe thanks to the Grand Portage National Monument in collaboration with the North House Folk School.

The last hours of the Edmund Fitzgerald

IT WAS NIGHT ON THE HARBOR A fog bank had rolled in from Superior. I was in the pilothouse of an old tugboat, chatting with the captain when three loud horn blasts startled me. A wall of steel came out of the mists and glided past our bow. It was an ore boat beginning her long voyage.

"That's the entryway the *Fitzgerald* used on her last voyage," the tugboat captain said.

I recalled my history: "It was a sunny, bright day in the harbor," I said. "A little muggy. The forecast called for thunderstorms later. Maybe big ones. So why'd she go?"

The captain thought for a moment. "They thought they could beat the storm."

November 9, 1975, had been unseasonably warm, and picture-perfect with the muggy heat that most mariners know in their hearts that something is about to happen. The weather forecast was for storms later, but weather on Superior was always unpredictable. Besides, the *Fitz* was topped up with a full load of iron ore, and she was steaming out fast.

"The crew was still fastening hatch covers as they left port."

The captain shook his head: "Nothing new. They often do that to save time on a calm day, and they fasten them at their leisure out to sea."

I nodded—nothing out of the ordinary there.

Her death, about a day later, is still disputed. And about a half-century later, it is still a mystery.

By the time she sailed out of the Superior entryway on her last voyage, she was not a new boat but a well-tested veteran. Her 729-foot keel was laid in 1958; she was the first maximum-sized freighter built up to that time and was for a while the largest freighter on the Great Lakes. She broke records for speed (up to 16 mph.) and for the tonnage she carried in her three cargo holds. I saw her many times as she steamed past the unused boathouse I lived in along the north shore outside Duluth.

On the waterfront, there were concerns about her "loose keel." Part of the ore carrier's keel had come loose from her bottom plates, and in an intense storm, the crew complained that they could see the longboat spring from side to side. The motion alarmed them and the noises it made.

Still, she had done this for years. The *Fitzgerald* was on her last run of the season. Then she could go back to the boatyard.

The *Fitz* had loaded in Duluth in about 4 hours, and the crew began putting on the 21 watertight hatches. They were of a clamshell design that called for a raised coaming that closed with a topside hatch that fit over it. The more water that came aboard, the harder the top hatch pressed down on the hatch coaming. The 5/16ths-inch thick steel hatches measuring 11 feet by 48 feet were so heavy at 14,000 pounds each that it took a permanent deck-mounted crane to open and close them. Each hatch cover was secured by two dozen special clamps. In her lifetime of service, she never arrived in port with any water damage in her cargo holds. She was the Queen of the Lakes.

Hatch covers were blamed for the *Fitzgerald's* sinking on November 10, but not everyone agreed. One night in the Apostle Islands, at anchor in *Persistence* behind an island, I studied the Coast Guard report investigating the *Fitzgerald's* sinking. I was surprised that the report cited not a single cause of the sinking but several causes, including failure of the hatch covers. In a brief cover letter introducing the report, a Coast Guard commandant singled out the hatch cover design as the sole cause of the *Fitz's* demise. That caused a fuss since other vessels use the same hatch cover design. I studied the lake carrier's response to the Coast Guard report, citing that the *Fitz* was equipped with the latest type of hatch covers and that she never arrived in port with water in her cargo or holds. Their boats also used this hatch design, and none of them leaked or sank.

I opened my forward hatch on *Persistence* to let in a little fresh breeze. This home-built wooden hatch is at the front of the cabin, and it is also a clamshell design. I have stuffed *Persistence's* bow into waves, with green water rolling up and over the hatch, and I have never had water leak below. I would know this first-hand. Below the hatch, I have my bunk. I never went to sleep on a wet bunk.

Before its sinking, the *Fitz* did not report any damage to its hatch covers. Only after passing over Six Fathom Shoals, Capt. McSorley reported fence rail down, broken vents, and, most telling of all, that his vessel had developed a sudden list. These details were the way one captain told another sea captain what was going wrong. On a boat the length of several football fields, the sudden list was a major indicator of severe damage.

But there was no mention of hatch cover damage. The *Fitz* captain only had to look out his aft window to look. He had done that to report the other damage.

The *Fitz* and the following *Anderson* were on the northern trek, customary for the big ore boats to travel to get shelter from the storm. The area they were headed for was well known to them, and one they passed near many times. An old ore boat, the *Irwin*, a museum ship in Duluth harbor, had in its pilothouse a chart of the area. In the chart's center was a big red ink mark in Six Fathom Shoals. Danger. Stay away, the mark was saying. No navigator could miss it. All captains knew of it.

But that's where the *Fitz* found a "new" reef. Its identity and location were added to marine navigation charts only after a Canadian survey identified it the following spring. When I ordered my charts for wilderness cruising in Canadian waters, I got a Canadian chart for every area of Superior. Onboard, I carried 28 full-size paper charts. The "new reef" was shown on a small paste-on tab of paper over the Caribou Island area.

Located among a cluster of reefs with soundings of 8 (24 feet) and 9 fathoms (27 feet), the "new reef" is only five ¼ fathoms from the surface. This is shallow enough for an ore boat to bottom out in storm conditions. Even big boats bounce up and down in high waves, sometimes moving as much as 7 to 10 feet. The *Fitz* drew 27 feet at the bow and 27 ½ feet at the stern. That means in a big wave, the *Fitz's* bow could have been lofted, then smashed down on a reef only 17 feet from the surface. And that is what ripped out her bottom. In a storm, she got too close.

There still might be evidence of a collision. If a 729-foot steel ship carrying 26,117 tons of taconite had smashed into a reef, the vessel must have left something behind. There would be the cataclysmic impact of the steel smashing upon the rock. The keel would scrape parts of the rock and bright rock would appear. Chips of rock would be knocked off. In places, there might be a gouge in the dark scum and growth that covers underwater rocks.

The steel hull would have left other evidence. The *Fitz's* bottom paint would have been scraped off on the reef, leaving streaks of color. From her torn bottom plates, there might have been metal pieces lying about. Maybe taconite pellets erupted from her ruptured hull.

There is a sequence of events worth noting. Before she went into that area, the *Fitz* had no problems; after she came out, she reported severe problems including a list, fence rail down, and broken vents—all indicators could only mean she had hit something. The reef was the only thing in her way to hit.

I asked a veteran mariner if the aft section crew knew of their danger, and he told me that if you live on a ship the way they did, they would know everything about her. The engine room crew would have heard and felt the impact of the steel hull on the reef. They could feel the hull listing over, and they stood on a sloping engine room floor. The crew could hear water gurgling in at an alarming rate and slamming unabated through the inadequate mesh bulkheads. They heard the *Fitz's* massive pumps, all of them, howling as they lost their fight against the rising water. As the ship listed further and sank lower in the water, they heard the waves boarding her spar deck. They saw water come below into the engine room and cause the overheated engine to steam up. Belowdecks, their situation must have been hellish.

At one point, the *Fitzgerald's* captain was overheard on the VHF radio yelling at his men on the aft section, ordering them to go below. I asked what that meant and the old captain's face grew thoughtful: "They were trying to get off."

The crew was struggling in freezing water to get to their lifeboat and launch it in monstrous waves. It was a near impossibility that lifeboats could live out there. It was also a remarkable but misguided effort: ore boat crews have the motto that the only time you go to your lifeboat is when you have to step up.

There are visions that haunt me. What happened in those fateful moments after the bow dug into a wave and did not rise again—but began a steep descent into the dark depths. The *Fitz* plunged downward at a speed of about 30 mph until it smashed at an angle into the bottom mud to a depth of 25 feet, then jolted forward. Inch-thick steel twisted and ruptured in the *Fitzgerald's* hull. Twenty-six thousand tons of taconite pellets exploded forward, burst the screen bulkheads, and slammed out like a shotgun blast. The 253-foot long aft section separated from the hull and torqued over to turn upside down on the bottom. In the cold and dark, the aft-section crew faced the horror of every sailor: trapped deep underwater with no hope of escape.

AFTERWORD

Years later, the wilderness area I admired and sailed through was enacted into being the Lake Superior National Marine Conservation Area (LSNMC). It is now the largest freshwater marine protected area in the world.

Spanning over one million hectares of Lake Superior, the LSNMC includes the lake, lakebed, islands, and north shorelands of Superior within its 10,000-square kilometer (3,860-mile) boundaries. It extends from Thunder Cape at the tip of Sleeping Giant Provincial Park in the west, to Bottle Point, just east of Terrace Bay, and south to Lake Superior's Canada-U.S. boundary.

In its southern waters, the conservation area links to the US Isle Royale National Park, an island in the middle of western Lake Superior famous for its rugged inlets and coves, shipwrecks, and isolated populations of wolves and moose. To the north, the conservation zone anchors already protected lands and waters, including the Nipigon River, known for its world-record speckled trout and woodland caribou. Supporters of the new park include Britain's Duke of Edinburgh and the World Wildlife Fund (WWF).

A one-time canoe guide in the area, Monte Hummel of WWF, celebrated the opening: "The waters, shoreline, and islands of Lake Superior are among the most rugged and pristine in the world, their beauty celebrated by painters such as Canada's Group of Seven, and their history captured in songs by Canadian icon, Gordon Lightfoot."

"It's a great day for peregrine falcons, eagles, osprey, bears, wolves, caribou and of course, those deep cold-water fish like lake trout, whitefish, and walleye that school in the (lake's) sparkling clear water unparalleled anywhere."

I talked to a Canadian boating friend of mine. "So has it changed?" I asked. "Are there barbed wire fences and Mounties guarding the gates?"

"Naw," he said. "It's pretty much the way you found it. Wilderness. And we want to keep it that way."

INDEX

ЭUT THE AUTHOR

Marlin Bree is an award-winning marine journalist and the author of many boating books, including *In the Teeth of the Northeaster*, *Wake of the Green Storm*, the *Boat Log & Record*, *Dead on the Wind*, and *Broken Seas*. He co-authored *Alone Against the Atlantic* with Gerry Spiess. His books are sold in bookstores, Internet booksellers, and marine distributors. Marlin's books are distributed to the book trade in the United States by IPG Books, Chicago, and are available in trade paperback form, e-books, and as pdf's. Some are available as audiobooks. He is a member of Boating Writers International and The Author's Guild. His website, **www.marlinbree.com** contains details and photos of the author's home-built boat, *Persistence*, and shows some of his boat building and maintenance tips. Also shown in color are scenic locations in which the author has sailed *Persistence*. To contact the author, you can reach him through e-mail: **marlinbree5@gmail.com.**

Marlin Bree and the *Persistence*.
Photo Will Bree